MANIFESTO FOR MISFITS

Brimming with creative inspiration, how-to projects, and useful information to enrich your everyday life, quarto.com is a favourite destination for those pursuing their interests and passions.

First published in 2022 by White Lion Publishing, an imprint of The Quarto Group.
The Old Brewery, 6 Blundell Street
London, N7 9BH, United Kingdom
T (0)20 7700 6700
www.quarto.com

A catalogue record for this book is available from the British Library.

ISBN 978-0-7112-6779-4
Ebook ISBN 978-0-7112-6781-7

10 9 8 7 6 5 4 3 2 1

Design by Leonardo Collina

Printed in China

Sink The Pink's

MANIFESTO
FOR
MISFITS

BE DIFFERENT, BE FREE, BE YOU

FOREWORD BY LILY ALLEN

GLYN FUSSELL

WHITE LION
PUBLISHING

FOREWORD

Sink The Pink has always been a very special place to me.

At their weird and wonderful events, everyone is welcome, celebrated and safe. Glyn and his troupe of gender-screwing, transgressive misfits are the embodiment of freedom of expression and fun. Their mission is and has always been to create a colourful world of unfettered joy, one that is truly inclusive and one where just about everything is possible, it's like walking into Narnia.

The misfit revolution starts with this book. With every page, we learn to embrace who we are and change the world to be a kinder, more interesting place. We inch closer to self-acceptance, from working out what makes us happy and harnessing the power of loving your differences, to reflecting on the hard times and exploring how to help ourselves and others along this journey. Glyn and the entire Sink The Pink family have lived it all and are exactly the outrageously divine cheerleaders we need.

This euphoric manifesto is a love letter to anyone who has ever felt like they don't belong. Channel its punk wisdom and you will feel brave enough to challenge ugly norms, uncomfortable truths and impossible expectations. You will learn that you are enough and then some, that you do belong, that you can dream big. And at the end of this extraordinary journey, you will wear your misfit label with pride.

Lily Allen

At the end of this extraordinary journey, you will wear your misfit label with pride.

INTRODUCTION

There are endless ways to be a misfit.

Sometimes, it's about your personality. Perhaps you're always told you're not 'cool' or 'normal' enough to fit in with the cool kids, or you've got your own quirky habits, tastes and mannerisms that other people just can't seem to wrap their heads around. On the other hand, it can also be about your identity. Whether it's the colour of your skin, the size and shape of your body or even who you're attracted to, there are plenty of markers of a 'misfit' – and according to the word's dictionary definition, there's something about us that the world finds 'uncomfortable'.

Millions of us have been tarred with the 'misfit' brush, told that we're 'different' and we don't 'fit in'. Being treated as the odd one out meant that for years I wanted nothing more than to become invisible, but for many of us misfits that may not be an option. Whether our differences are visible or not, bullies always seem to sniff out something to pick on. We're often treated as scapegoats and punch-bags by people desperate to punch down at someone, so we end up moving through life feeling hyper-visible, like we can't escape. Once you've been labelled a misfit, you're relentlessly framed as 'other', not just by those who are desperate to drag you down but by media, society and sometimes even your loved ones.

The world tells you to conform by shapeshifting into someone you're not, and aspire to chase dreams and achieve goals that hold absolutely no meaning for you.

Let Your Freak Flag Fly

If there's something rooted deep within your character that makes other people uncomfortable, that's not your fault. The world needs to accommodate and celebrate that difference. No matter how tempting it might sometimes feel, trying to 'fix' parts of yourself that were never broken in the first place can have serious long-term consequences. Think about the pain of queer conversion therapy, or the very real dangers of skin-bleaching, or the mental strain of constantly policing your own behaviour to make other people happy. Trying to become something you aren't is an idea that plenty of us misfits, exhausted, have toyed with at some point, but trust me when I say it does more harm than good.

I always felt the sting of difference first-hand. Nobody ever expected too much from me. I was always the kid that everyone discounted, so for the longest time even *I* didn't really believe in myself. Sometimes, life just seems to cement your failures, right? Here are some of mine:

- I left school with two GCSE qualifications – to get into a good college, you're supposed to have five.
- When I did get into college, I was kicked out for always being lost in my own dream world.
- I've been sacked from nearly every job I've ever had.
- I was a failed teenage 'model' – yes, really!
- I worked as a hotel singer in Ayia Napa.

However, I proved them all wrong once I found the place I could truly shine: Sink The Pink. Now, we're kicking ass on a global scale and achieving things nobody ever expected of us.

- We have performed around the world, from New York to Singapore, Berlin to Sydney.
- I became creative director for a Spice Girl! and released a single inspired by the club.
- I launched the biggest LGBTQ+ music festival in Europe, Mighty Hoopla.
- I co-created – alongside my wonderful partner in crime Amy Zing – the most successful queer club brand in the last decade, which still shines brightly.
- The Sink The Pink gang have been on magazine covers and have been shot by legendary fashion photographers such as Nick Knight and David Bailey.
- Basically, I've become a bloody queer icon babes!

SPREAD THE POSITIVITY WORLDWIDE

Now, I'm on a mission. I've realised that most of what marked me as different is what made me successful – my wild imagination, my bold personality, the refusal to be told what to do – and now, the label 'misfit' is one I happily use to describe myself. If I can rid the term 'misfit' of its old, negative connotations, I reckon you can do the same. In fact, I challenge you to reclaim it as something punk and beautiful: a descriptor that you embrace whole-heartedly.

Be a Proud Misfit

It's been a rough ride, but I can proudly say that I now move through life surrounded by a pack of fellow glamorous weirdos, and we all wear our 'misfit' label as a badge of honour. Self-acceptance and pride give us permission to free ourselves from social dictates and tired narratives. Our gloriously weird drag collective, Sink The Pink, brings joy, hilarity and radiance into my life, and together we spread that positivity worldwide.

I managed to get through without internalising the idea that I was *too much,* or that I should be less, or that I should follow the conventional route to success. I have had years of hard knocks and experience figuring out how to be authentically myself, and that's the place this book comes from. I've found that most self-help guides and workbooks fail to reckon with what it truly means to be a 'misfit', not to mention the emotional baggage which that label can bring. The world so often sees it as a crease to be ironed out, as something to change. But not in this book, baby! From my earliest years, my dreams and ambitions were rooted in my desire to move through life as a weirdo and reshape what that meant on my own terms. So, I'll take you back to my childhood and give you a glimpse into the cringiest parts of my own brain.

Hopefully, my trip down memory lane will encourage you to peer deep into your own beautiful brain and unlock those wacky concepts that might end up becoming your life's work. Maybe you've got a super-niche interest that could end up becoming the love of your life when you learn to embrace and nurture it without shame. Perhaps, like me, you're so tired of feeling excluded or not catered to within the world as it currently is that you dive into the kaleidoscopic corners of your imagination and create something of your own – not just to bring yourself joy, but to bring it to others like you as well.

The Building Blocks

You'll learn the power of reframing, creating alter egos and building new worlds. These are drag queen staples, but it turns out that they work pretty fabulously for pop stars and the rest of us mere mortals too. You'll look into what makes you uniquely *you*, rummage around to find all those rough diamonds and then make them sparkle, even on your roughest days. You'll also explore joy and happiness: what are they, how can we actively chase them and what messages do we need to unlearn in order to get there?

Of course, there's no point in sugar-coating everything and acting like life will never be difficult. As a misfit, there are a few dark forests that you'll have to run through – complete with verbal, ideological and mental obstacles – to reach your own paradise. You'll find ways to overcome those struggles and use them to fuel your transformation into a fully-fledged, sparkling misfit butterfly. Only after you've worked through all that bullshit can you truly start taking a creative approach to figuring out the mark you want to leave on the world.

Each epiphany will teach you more about yourself, and in turn, they'll all lead you in the direction of other mind-blowingly brilliant weirdos. You'll run into new communities, allies and friends, and whether they're part of your online knitting group or they're with you on the sweaty dance floor of a club gazing lovingly into your eyes, these like-minded people will make any storm easier to weather.

After this unlearning, reframing and rethinking, you'll be pretty fucking bored of all the systems working to keep us feeling like our 'misfit' status is something to be ashamed of. So what do we do? Crush them! Whether it's by building your own communities rooted in mutual aid, finding trailblazers to campaign with or absorbing the skills and confidence you need to stamp your mark on archaic institutions, there's plenty you can do to chew up existing systems and spit them out into something resembling your own revolution. We've all got the power, and the biggest lie we're sold is that we can't tap into it unless we're willing to conform. This book and the resilient, charismatic weirdos within it are here to say: Fuck That! Together, we're living proof that weirdos well and truly can win in the end.

PINKY PROMISE

Let me start by thanking you for arriving at this book.

Like you, at times, I have felt like a complete nobody. I've felt invisible, worthless. It felt like there was no space in this whole wide world for me to be me. And even when I didn't feel it, I was told it.

Fast forward a couple of decades. I've run into everything I've been afraid of and come out at the other side singing, dancing and high-kicking the haters. It wasn't always that way, though; I used to be frozen by fear and anxiety. I was that boy who went scarlet when anyone spoke to him, and I would visibly shake when I had to step into a social situation. I used to be terrified of standing out in a crowd or using my voice, yet now I spend my life standing in front of thousands of people onstage in killer heels and a wig! I speak publicly to organisations and businesses as a consultant, I stand up for everything I believe in and, when I'm out in public, I'm nothing short of a human firework.

I've learned to confront fear head-on, and it's a lesson that's changed my life. I've even learned to love myself, and the good news is that you can feel this way too. That is my pinky promise to you: I and my amazing gang of social misfits and broken biscuits will share everything we've learned on our journeys to help you through yours.

We all know through first-hand experience that there's real joy to be found in confounding preconceived expectations, understanding our worth and carving our own paths in life without letting go of the qualities we've been wrongly bullied and harassed for. Think of us as your cheerleaders: we'll tell you why *you* deserve better, and how you can find yourself, your joy, your home and your people, so that you can tap into that same self-love and self-understanding.

Trust me, when society, with its fixation on endless boring rules, boxes and labels, treats you like a misfit, cheerleaders are essential. Everyone sharing their story in this book can relate to feeling like an outsider. All of us were told at some point that we had to compromise, change and shrink ourselves to match someone else's definitions and ideas of happiness.

So, who the hell am I? I'm the co-founder of Sink The Pink, a world-famous drag troupe that roams the globe recruiting new misfits through our all-singing, all-dancing entertainment extravaganzas. We're a leading force when it comes to inclusive nightlife, and we do it all in ridiculous DIY dresses with an enormous zest for life! I'm not a therapist and I'm certainly not a PhD-juggling darling of the academe, but I *am* a human being who has struggled, lived and then thrived on unlocking and embracing the misfit in myself, as well as those around me. I have built a career based on pure, unapologetic joy, and nurtured a queer, drag ecosystem that continues to spread its roots. Now, I'm here to nurture you too – shrieking with pride as you work through this book and learn to unlock this unapologetic streak within yourself.

Throughout all of this, I've learned once and for all that being a misfit isn't something to overcome, no matter what anyone leads you to believe. In fact, the opposite is true – we're here to tell you that it's something to be cherished, embraced and celebrated. By the end of this wild, wonderful journey, you'll feel proud to let your freak flag fly. That's our pinky promise to you.

CHAPTER 1

YOU'VE GOT THE

POW

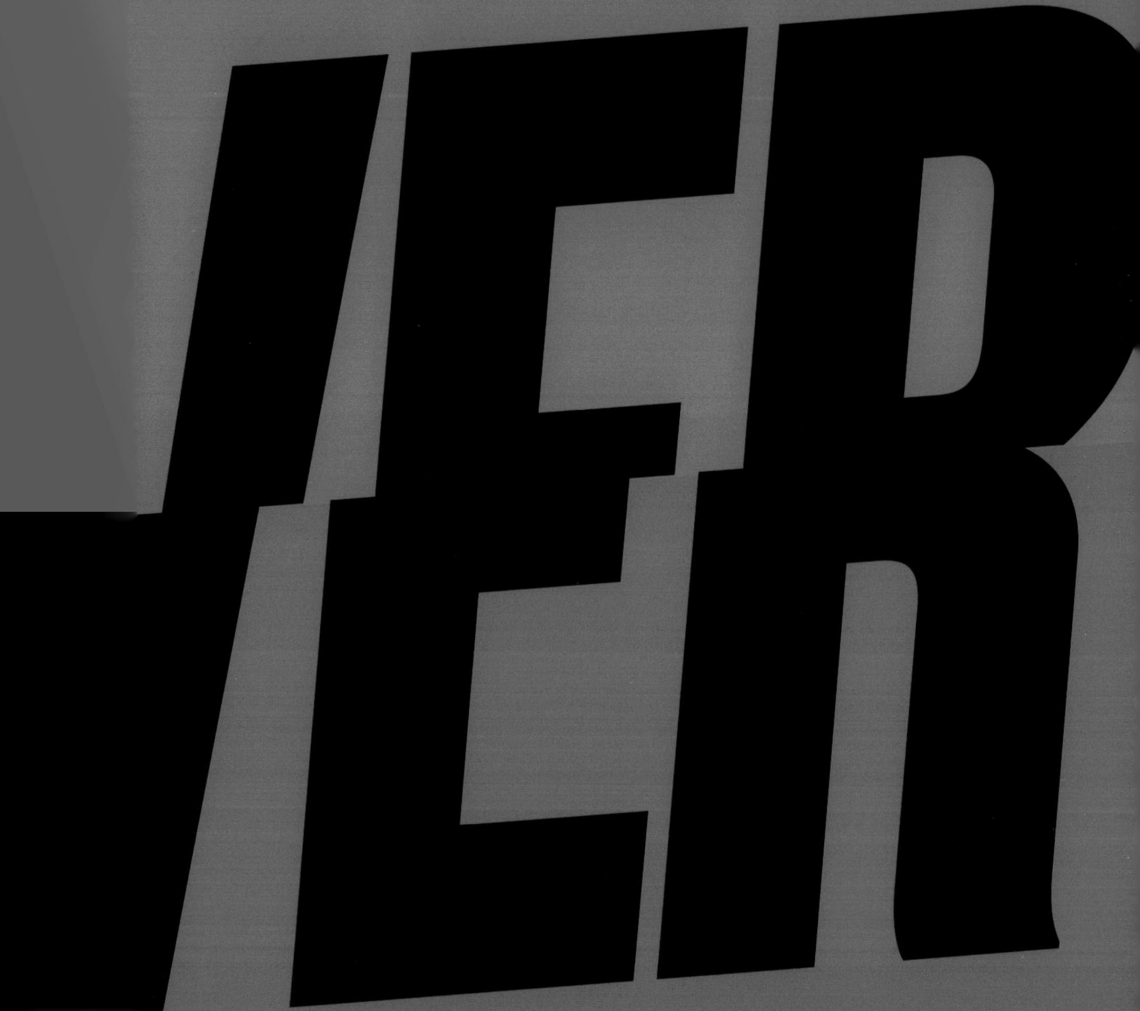

RECLAIM THE WORD

'MISFIT'

So often, the word 'misfit' is intended to be shrouded in negativity, a burden – and although the road for each and every one of us is totally different, that word and that sometimes unshakeable feeling of difference can follow us. As a shy, queer kid, the last thing I wanted was that label – but over time, I've embraced it. Now, I love it.

I wish I had understood the strength of my individuality from a young age. Growing up with six siblings in innercity Bristol, my childhood home was totally chaotic. From fights and tantrums to laughter and games, there was always something going on, which made it difficult to speak openly and at length about how alienated I sometimes felt by the word 'misfit'. There were plenty of good times, but on bad days, I spent a lot of time hiding in the curtains, trying desperately to ignore how much of a weirdo the world made me feel.

It's not just me, either. You, dear reader, likely have countless experiences of your own to look back at; the days you were made to feel like an outcast. Sometimes, we're made to feel excluded for factors we can't control. Maybe it's your race, gender or sexuality that gets weaponised against you. Perhaps it's your weight, your mental health condition, your neurodivergence. Being too quiet, too loud, too 'different' – whatever the hell that means – can all earn us labels like 'misfit', intended as insults to break us down or force us into states of perennial self-censorship.

Learning to Love Yourself

Now visibly an out-and-proud extrovert, people always trip over their jaw in shock when I tell them I was ridiculously shy as a child. I sometimes felt I was so delicate that I might actually break in half; like I had been born into a world that I was in no way prepared for or equipped to deal with. I've always been surrounded by mayhem, which means that now I'm suited, booted and ready to handle any madness that comes my way.

When I was younger, dealing with life felt debilitating. I'm sure you know the feeling – that knot in your stomach on the first day of school, the jolt of panic when you see a bully eyeing you up, even the heat of embarrassment that flashes across your body when you're laughed at for saying the wrong thing. I spent years being terrified of being tripped up or told off, and throughout that period, I felt almost permanently scared and vulnerable, like my differences were a target painted across my back. It's a familiar feeling for all of us misfits; the sense that if only we could conform, we'd be secure.

Yet as the years have passed, I've learned to love the little oddball I see in the mirror. I've learned to embrace all of my peculiarities too, like the obsession with Lycra that led me to start a local wrestling club, or the laser-focused determination I had to create my own range of perfumes from household smells – as it turns out, not such a great idea! I even managed to clutch a few of the strange, wacky quirks that earned me the 'misfit' tag and recognise them as integral parts of my character. I certainly wouldn't be the bollock-flashing, loud-mouthed weirdo I am now if I hadn't clung onto my love of dressing up to make myself look as scary as possible, and I *definitely* wouldn't be selling out venues if I hadn't allowed myself to keep writing my monthly musicals!

Inhabit Your Space

I grew up in a working-class area where everyone played by the rules, did exactly what they were told to do – not just because society says so, but because it was often what was needed to survive. Deep down, I was a creative, flamboyant gay kid who wanted to dress up and run straight into the unknown, but on the outside I seemed quiet, shy and insecure. Yet, around my family in particular, I was theatrical with a zany, sometimes disgusting imagination. My childhood was spent inventing games and challenges for my family – once, the game involved sticking hose-pipes up our bums and seeing how far we could run before the water fell out! Then there was the time – and not to brag! – that I pioneered the 'vajazzle', by challenging my family members to create arts-and-crafts masterpieces on their private parts.

On these few occasions when I did come out of my shell, I would end up being told regularly that I was 'too much', 'too weird' or just flat-out gross.

Although I wanted nothing more than to step into my mum's dresses and strut down to my local corner shop like a flouncy, ebullient peacock, I learned to dial down my differences to make myself more palatable. I wasn't ready to step into my fabulousness and wear it as a badge of honour back then. Maybe you aren't yet either, and that's okay – for plenty of us misfits, it feels like every statement of self-expression will earn us some kind of punishment.

You likely feel forced to do this too, no matter what that means to you. Perhaps your timidity makes you feel guilty about being an introvert, or the omnipresent and so often unspoken rules of social conduct feel like a code you're constantly being told you haven't quite cracked. Whether we're being told what – or what not – to wear or how to adjust our behaviour around relatives, there's plenty of guilt-tripping and name-calling that goes into keeping us quiet. Back then, I allowed it to happen because I wasn't brave or wise enough to realise the qualities that marked me as a 'misfit' made me a beautiful flamingo in a sea of

TOO WEIRD GROSS QUEER MUCH.

boring, homogenous beige. Whether you are a flamboyant flamingo or a quiet but awesome oddball, you too can be brave enough to inhabit your space with confidence.

Back then, I definitely wasn't strong enough to reclaim the labels that were used against me. It's been a real process to come to terms with everything that makes me a misfit; it's bigger than my sexuality, my appearance or my slightly peculiar personality. It's all the traits that mark us out as 'weird' or 'different' that truly make us wonderful. Like you, dear reader, I am and will always be one of life's oddities.

SOCIETY
FEARS
OUR

When someone says you're 'too much', what they really mean is that they don't know what to do with you, they can't quite place what box to put you in. That's not your problem; it's theirs. Despite this fact, we misfits often spend our early years being punished for stepping out of line. We see it all the time, across almost all demographics.

Sometimes, this goes beyond the individual. It becomes discrimination, the kind that we need to openly acknowledge and work to fix. Black children, for example, are subjected to discriminatory uniform policies that forbid them from wearing protective hairstyles in class. In 2019, Michelle De Leon and Denese Chikwendu, Directors of World Afro Day CIC, authored a 'Hair Equality Report'[1,] that found one in six black children in the UK had had a bad school experience because of their natural hair texture. Elsewhere, we see schools banning hijabs[2] and ignoring playground discrimination. None of this is restricted to the UK, either – in countries across the world, restrictive policies force budding misfits to shrink themselves or repress themselves entirely, especially in the case of trans children, so often caught in the crossfire of political arguments and discrimination masked as 'concern' by parents and teachers.[3]

It's hard to truly articulate how much of a toll this bullshit can take on our souls. I grew up in the era of Section 28, a right-wing law which banned the 'promotion' – an obvious dog whistle (the kind of discriminatory language so coded it's easy to miss, especially for readers with less understanding of marginalised communities) – of homosexuality in UK schools. It made for a bizarre combination: on the streets, where I was harassed, I felt hyper-visible, yet in school curriculums across the country, my community was literally invisible, erased from history as if we were some kind of eyesore. The homophobic stigma perpetuated by the media throughout the AIDS crisis still lingered too; even when I was a teenager, coming out as gay in 1999 was seen as a death sentence.

So, how the hell do we work through all of this to truly embrace ourselves despite this barrage of hurdles?

LEARN FROM
Past MISFITS

←——————————————

Falling in love with the word 'misfit' wasn't easy, but I urge you to look to past trailblazers who have taught us that there's strength in reclaiming insults on your own terms.

Throughout history, activists have taken words used to break them down and reclaimed them, changing their definition by embracing them openly. The word 'queer' is a great example. It's been around since the sixteenth century, and initially it just meant strange or peculiar. Then, in 1894, it was used as a gay slur for the first time in the midst of a salacious sex scandal: upon finding out his son was sleeping with a man, John Douglas, ninth Marquess of Queensberry, wrote a letter[4] describing them both as 'snob queers'. His son also enjoyed dalliances with Oscar Wilde (honestly, goals) and as a result the letter later surfaced during Oscar Wilde's trial, and the pejorative descriptor stuck.

The radical activists of Queer Nation, who fought the US government for its homophobic mishandling of the AIDS Crisis, reclaimed the term. In a blistering manifesto[5] written by anonymous members and passed around a 1990 Pride march in New York, they stated: 'When a lot of lesbians and gay men wake up in the morning we feel angry and disgusted, not gay. So we've chosen to call ourselves queer.' The ballsy protest group continued to use 'queer' for maximum impact, writing statement slogans like 'Queers Bash Back' which sent shockwaves through the LGBT+ community, whose previous attempts at activism had often been pretty mild-mannered. While more conservative campaigners politely requested change, Queer Nation preferred to smash down the door and demand it.

In that same spirit, I proudly describe myself as 'queer' because I see it as an unapologetic 'Fuck You!' to the idea that we need to be boxed into oppositional labels like 'gay' and 'straight'. By comparison, queer is limitless; it cracks open the bland, boring ideas of 'normality' that kept me down as a kid, so I grabbed that word years ago, and I still scream it from the rooftops.

Of course, I can see why the term still raises eyebrows – I'm part of a generation that grew up being pelted with that word as a slur, and it's understandable that some find it hard to move past that. Similarly, it's your choice to identify however you like: toy with labels and see what sticks for you. There's power to be gained by claiming these terms as your own, but it's a journey that takes time and ultimately looks different for everyone. All I know is that, for me, the word 'queer' felt like a rejection of shame and a statement of power.

Although it's not a slur, I believe we should do the same for the term 'misfit'. There are some pretty key similarities: look in the dictionary, and you'll find that both are used as synonyms for weird, strange and unnatural, which I now think are my best qualities, thank you very much.

Just as activists reclaimed queerness on their own terms, I wear my misfit label with pride. It's my own personal mission to make you all love the word as much as I now do.

FAKE IT 'TIL YOU MAKE IT MAKE IT MAKE IT

Context is important here. Obviously, I can't wander into NASA and blag my way through a spaceship repair (although I'd love to try). For me, it was less about faking a skillset than it was about performing behaviour. If you practise the performance of confidence, people gradually start to treat you differently over time. Maybe they take your ideas more seriously, or they slowly start to understand that you're not someone to be messed with.

It's helpful to remind yourself that who you are now is not who you'll be in ten years' time, or even ten days' time. Personalities and characters are fluid and malleable; if you intentionally set out who you want to become, there's a good chance you'll get there.

I spent years developing the habit of convincing myself that I was confident, that I could achieve whatever I wanted. I would repeat these affirmations in my head whenever the nasty, negative voices that threatened to drag me away from my potential crept into my mind. It wasn't always easy and I didn't always succeed, but creating and then practising this ritual is what counted. Soon enough, I did it without thinking and I realised that I was actually living these changes rather than just yearning for them.

We're raised in a world that drills into us the idea that there's such a thing as 'normal', or even – God forbid – perfect. These ideas are all constructs but understanding that doesn't make overcoming them feel like any less of an impossible mountain to climb.

Instead of trying to scale that mountain in one night, think about each day as your chance to take another step in the direction of total self-acceptance. Focus on the small changes that can gently push you outside of your comfort zone. Try to take a small leap of faith with me. Think of me and the fabulous voices in this book as your own cheerleaders. I know for a fact that it's a mentality that works. At Sink The Pink, we've had the joy of watching beautiful weirdos feel free to be the biggest, most unapologetically brilliant versions of themselves. They all had that potential within them, and you do too.

SOMETIᴍES, ALL IT TAKƎS

You don't have to create a fabulous drag persona, but there is real power to be found in dressing up.

We know this already – think about agonising over your perfect prom look, or meticulously picking out a job interview outfit to dazzle your potential employers. For clubbers, it's basically a sacred ritual: slapping on your war paint, teasing your hair to the heavens (the higher the hair, the closer to God!) and slipping into something you know is guaranteed to make jaws drop on the dance floor. Our clothes send a message to the world about who we are and what we stand for, but they can also act as a vehicle to help us present the self we see inside, or at least the one we want to project.

Even as a shy kid, I always knew I had it in me to be a little bit extra. When I learned about Tudor history at ten years old, I was floored by the drama, the britches, the ruffs! I wrote an entire musical about Henry VIII. Naturally, I played the leading role and stepped into the character of a maniacal villain chasing everyone around the stage wielding a fake axe. This was my first taste of onstage drama. Later in life, I channelled this same chaotic energy into a gloriously messy, balls-out drag character called Glynfamous, who helped me to truly come out of my shell.

As a kid learning to express myself, dressing up helped, and so did letting loose and being theatrical. Drag isn't just an art form, it's a state of mind. It's about giving yourself permission to truly not give a fuck, and embracing all the qualities that you're always told to downplay or silence in case they're not palatable. Words can chip away at us as we move through life, shrinking us into boxes which feel impossible to break out of. Creating an alter ego gives you back your voice, offering a vehicle for self-expression that can push you to do the things that you might fear. To illustrate this point, I'm going to turn to a handful of Sink The Pink's colourful queer family to show just how empowering it can be.

IS AN _____ ALTER EGO

Raven Mandella

I spent my teenage years being made to feel shit about myself. I've been bullied, told I'm worthless. But my mum inspired my strength, my courage and my drag persona. The way I see it, Raven Mandella is *everything* – why be just black or white when you have a whole spectrum to play with? So I embrace my masculinity and my femininity; I see the strength in them both and I fuse them together. My drag is me in my ultimate form.

Jonbenet Blonde

As a kid, I always wanted to be a Spice Girl. I made costumes out of blankets in my attic bedroom and started doing drag when I was sixteen years old; that got me kicked out of my family home. Drag was like my superhero costume; it empowered me and taught me how to own my sexuality, which is definitely something I never saw growing up in rural Ireland. It also led me to some amazing moments – I was onstage with bloody Mel C at Times Square! Genuinely, if I hadn't spent so much time surrounded by incredible queens, I wouldn't have had any hope at all. The minute I stepped into it was a lightbulb moment: A-ha, *this* is what I was meant to do!

Grace Shush

I don't know if this sounds conceited, but I always knew that I was meant for *something* – I remember thinking about that a lot, but growing up was traumatic. I really suffer with paranoia, and I really didn't have any friends until I was in my mid-teens. As a loner, all you ever want is for someone to want you, but I was this fat, gay weirdo. Actually, one of my earliest school memories is being choked by a kid. I created my drag characters as escapism, and I think – and this is so earnest and gross! – but if it wasn't for Grace Shush, I don't think I'd be here today. I was so ashamed of my body, so confused about my gender. Grace became this entirely different person, through which I could throw away those fears and become this fabulous, gorgeous character.

EVƎN SPICE GIRLS START SOMƎWHᴇRE

It's not just drag queens that swear by alter egos.

Even bona fide goddess Beyoncé needed a little help to become her best self, which came in the form of an onstage alter ego, Sasha Fierce. Whereas Beyoncé was a little more introvert, Sasha was more outspoken, more forthright and more sensual, and this was reflected in her onstage personality, outfits and breathless choreography. Stefani Germanotta took a similar approach and created Lady Gaga, the part of herself she calls the 'stronger individual'. With each of her albums Gaga has shapeshifted and created different looks that don't conform to the stereotypical ideals of feminine beauty expected of female popstars. Often her looks make statements about herself, her music or show support for repressed groups.

This might seem extreme, but it's way too easy to let our perceptions of ourselves get in the way. Before we have time to really understand the brilliance of our misfit qualities, we get trapped inside our own heads and block our own blessings. We lose sight of the fact that everyone starts somewhere.

That's where idols come into play. I know you've done it too – scrolled endlessly through facts about your favourite stars to pick out parts of their life stories that resonate with your own. Especially when you're at the start of your journey of self-discovery, seeing these fully realised yet flawed, complex characters can help to piece together the parts of your own identity and give you something to aspire to. Maybe it's their skill, creativity or ambition that draws you in, or it could be as simple as reflecting your values and amping them up – either way, it's these aspirational stars that can give us strength on even the shittiest of days.

It's not all about celebrities, either. Research[6] shows that role models – whether famous or not – can be particularly helpful for teens figuring out their own path in life, but more generally, our own personal heroes can play a key role in helping us figure out who we want to be. Maybe their stories mirror ours, and seeing their happy endings and the road to get there can give us ideas for managing chaos in our own life; it could simply be the case that the coping mechanisms or realisations they describe resonate with us on some level. Whatever the reason, finding your own positive role models can be hugely beneficial when honing the resilience to move through life as a misfit.

As I've grappled with my own journey of self-acceptance, I've been lucky enough to meet some of my idols and learn about their lives – and you might be surprised to hear that their lives are not always as glamorous or easy as you think.

Meeting Melanie C – AKA Sporty Spice – was a real full-circle moment for me. It zapped me straight back into that star-struck teenager who saw the Spice Girls as totally superhuman. They seemed almost otherworldly. So ferociously powerful and confident. Whenever I felt invisible or insecure, I turned to them for strength. They had this real magnetic presence, and it wasn't just me that felt it. Like millions of confused, lost kids around the world, I gravitated towards their energy on days when I couldn't summon up my own.

Just like the rest of us, she grew up grappling the internal struggles of learning to harness her potential as a misfit. Don't just take my word for it, though – here's a Spice Girl's story of finding power in a world that tries to strip it from us.

SO FEROCIOUSLY POWERFUL AND CONFIDENT

PHONE A FRIEND

MELANIE C

Glyn How much did the idea of being a misfit resonate with you growing up?

Melanie C A lot, mainly because my parents divorced when I was three or four years old. This was the late '70s. Everyone had parents who were still together, so it made me feel like the odd one out. They both re-married, but I'm the only child from their relationship. I felt like a spare part, a burden. I truly believe a lot of the drive I had to be successful came from needing to establish my own environment, one that I had created. It was about having my own place in the world.

Glyn These things can defeat some people, but you found strength in them. How did you do that?

Melanie C

The funny thing is that I immediately found a passion for performing when I got to do it. It's such a huge part of my identity that I felt like, 'Oh, this is my home!' But wanting to be successful at that also made me a misfit. I was bullied because I danced. My friends were the glee club kids who loved singing, dancing and acting, but I hardly had any others because I was bullied for taking ballet classes. In the working-class environment I grew up in, it was like, 'You think you're better than us – you're a snob!' But that passion was my strength.

Glyn

Take me back to auditioning for the Spice Girls. What was going on in your mind?

Melanie C

I got this grant to go to a performing arts college – thank God, my parents couldn't have afforded it – but when I left and started auditioning for shows, nothing was happening. I was going for chorus parts in musicals and not getting recalls, like what the fuck? I didn't even want to be in the fucking chorus, I wanted the lead role! Things weren't going well, but at an audition for a cruise, I was a handed a flyer for a girl band, and suddenly there was no doubt that's what I wanted to do.

I auditioned and got a recall, but I was ill – I had tonsillitis, I couldn't speak. My mum begged the management team and was told it was too late, but a few weeks later I got a phone call saying one of the other girls hadn't worked out. They wanted me to come in! I sang Stevie Wonder's 'Signed, Sealed, Delivered', and that was it. No big announcement, I was just in the band!

GIRL POWER!

Glyn **It feels almost like you were just riding the wave towards your destiny.**

 Melanie C Honestly! We were all very different, but we didn't really think about it; we just knew the chemistry was explosive. All of us tried dressing the same for a bit, but everyone just looked a bit silly so we started showing up dressed how we felt comfortable. That's how we started being given nicknames for our individuality, and that's what made us powerful. We were all misfits with our own backgrounds and stories, but it was magical to have these five totally different people come together.

Glyn **What was it about Sporty Spice that helped you unlock your power?**

Melanie C There's this real cultural strive for perfection, but we were so unapologetically flawed. There's this real fluidity within me. Growing up, I was feminine and I loved classical ballet, and even now I'm quite a gentle, graceful person, but I also love sport, and I can be very physical and outspoken. The Spice Girls allowed me to explore that fluidity within myself, and it's a mentality that's stayed with me – why should we have to conform to stereotypes? I fully embrace every aspect of myself in every role I play in my life, whether it's as a mum, a Spice Girl or a solo artist.

Glyn Finally, how do you keep all of this in check when your mind goes to darker places, or when you go through particularly shitty times?

Melanie C I do struggle with depression from time to time. The scariest thing is when you feel that fire in your belly has been put out, when you're not excited or enthusiastic about anything. We grow up in a society which expects us to achieve certain things at certain ages, but as you get older, you start to realise those milestones don't make you happy. Ninety-eight per cent of the time, I manage to remind myself of that and keep that fire in my belly alive. I know those moments will pass. I'm also constantly searching for my own joy, and I'm not embarrassed about that anymore! Finding those moments of your own happiness is the most important thing in life.

CREATE YOUR ALTER EGO

Your new alter-ego name should communicate whatever it is that you're aspiring to. Make it creative, larger-than-life and playful too – you want to hear the name and understand exactly what that alter ego's personality is like.

Where do they shop? How do they act? Think about the things and the places you love, about everything that makes you laugh, and go from there. I've been doing this for a long time for drag queens, so let me walk you through the process.

- Imagine you're a budget queen that loves rap music. You could be... Lidl Kim!
- Imagine you're a punky, Goth metal queen. I give you... Sue Gives a Fuck!
- A plus-size '80s fitness instructor queen? Jane Fondue!

It works for drag kings too...
- A muscled Adonis? Jim Bunny!
- A character who mocks male chauvinists? Step forward... Mel Privilege!

- Now it's your turn – and to get those mental cogs whirring, here are a few briefs to start you off...

- A science-loving, body-positive character...
- A Goth leather rocker...
- A brash, energetic go-getter...

Keep free-styling until you find the alter ego that fits! And know that it's okay to let them evolve over time.

LIVE THE LIFE YOU WANT

Society is *obsessed* with a before and after. We're fed never-ending success stories that sell us the idea that, with a few tweaks, we'll finally become happy.

We're told that we need to be thinner, taller, better looking, more masculine, more feminine, more normal; the list is endless. Usually, the solution involves buying a shitload of products, and in turn buying into the idea that who you currently are isn't quite *enough*.

The truth is that you already have all the power and potential you need. Those qualities that make you a misfit are ultimately your strength. Maybe your sensitivity is read as weakness, when in reality it's an attribute that makes you perfectly suited to becoming a force of good in the world, or a reliable shoulder to cry on for loved ones. Your out-there imagination might get you mocked in your everyday life, but it's the ticket to magnificent, mind-expanding brilliance that can only come from seeing the world through gloriously eccentric eyes. You don't need to wait to be any more or less anything; it's all about self-acceptance.

None of us unlock our potential straight away, and to some extent, life really is a journey – that shy, reserved kid could never have imagined the life I live today, one that's custom-built to embrace and celebrate everything that I was ever told made me 'too much'. In some way, the same will happen to you too. Once you learn to cast off the shackles of societal messaging and understand that what makes you a misfit is what makes you truly magnificent, you'll realise that, yes, you are allowed to dream of a life bigger and more fantastical than anything you could currently imagine. Step into your misfit magic and, over time, the world will just have to catch up.

STEP INTO YOUR MISFIT MAGIC

CHAPTER 2

DREA

M BIG

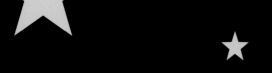

FIND YOUR
DREAM

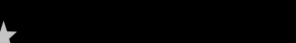

We've already established that society can be pretty unkind to us misfits, but why is that?

You might not always notice it, but each of us moves through the world governed by a series of downright odd rules that tell us all how we *should* look, act and behave. Like most of us misfits, I despised these 'social norms' from a young age.

These rules vary based on who you are, where you are and who you're surrounded by, but social norms beat into us the idea that we should conform to certain rules: boys wear blue, girls wear pink, anyone that doesn't adhere to the gender binary simply doesn't exist. They tell us that men should be assertive, stoic and aggressive, that women should be subservient, pliant and eager to please. Society is built around these premises. Think of how the widely accepted blueprint of a successful life – marriage, kids, a good career – is designed with cookie-cutter, heterosexual, traditional family set-ups in mind, and you'll start to understand why we misfits come up against so much backlash.

We're expected to conform, but doing so is a losing game when the rules were never built to apply to us.

I take absolute joy in sticking two fingers up to this system now, but first I had to learn a few lessons. The first is that 'normal' doesn't exist. These boxes and categories that we treat as so fixed, essential and immovable are all completely fictional. They have been created throughout history.

Did you know that 'homosexuals' didn't exist until the early twentieth century? It was only when sexologists – think of them as curious, bearded scholars determined to categorise sexual difference – began examining 'inverts', as homosexuals were then known, that we gained a language for sexuality. Before then, who you fucked was a matter of what you did as opposed to a statement of who you were.

Racial categories are similarly entrenched in societies worldwide, but the construct of 'whiteness' was initially created by tyrannical, wealthy landlords. They saw indentured European labourers building solidarity with enslaved African workers and knew they needed to divide them. As Emma Dabiri brilliantly outlined in *What White People Can Do Next*', it wasn't until the Barbados Slave Code of 1661 that white people were deemed 'white'. The language used in the code gave 'white' European labourers supremacy over their African counterparts, appeasing them enough to destroy any political interests they might have otherwise had in fighting for the same causes as the enslaved Africans.

Whiteness and supremacy have been interlinked from day one, and preserving the myth that race is a fixed, unchanging concept is essential to maintaining the status quo.

There is some solace to be found in the fact that social norms that keep misfits oppressed are completely fictional, and they change throughout history. With any luck, they'll nudge in a more progressive direction as we all continue to unlearn the toxic bullshit that's been drummed into us since birth. Without doubt, understanding these

We're expected to conform, but doing so is a losing game when the rules were never built to apply to us.

facts helped me realise there was nothing inherently wrong with me; I just didn't happen to fit the restrictive boxes that had somehow come to be seen as normal. Still, knowing this internal truth didn't make navigating life and discrimination any easier.

That's Where Dreaming Comes In

When I say 'dreaming', I don't mean treating yourself to six naps a day – although if that's what you need, then go ahead! For me, it has multiple meanings. There's daydreaming, which goes hand in hand with joy, imagination and creativity. Then, there's dreaming of a future that's built on your own terms. Often us misfits feel like our dreams (and the path to them) don't fit in with what's expected of us. This might mean pursuing a job purely because you enjoy it, rather than one where you know exactly what your career will look like over the next decade; or being child-free and unmarried by choice and enjoying the freedom that affords you; or knowing that you want to uproot your life and move abroad to somewhere you've always wanted to live.

Of course, there are endless political and societal barriers in the way – perhaps a lack of access to education or resources, or a lack of family support – but you don't have to abandon these dreams altogether just because you're told to. Shooting for the stars as a misfit usually means working twice as hard, but some of the perceived barriers are entirely subjective, and maybe your dreams are actually within reach after all. Perhaps you've just been conditioned to feel like you're not good enough, and if you can find a way to set those insecurities aside, you will be able to live your dreams after all.

All of this requires laser-sharp focus and ambitions that might seem lofty at first, but I promise that focus and ambition can pay off. I wouldn't be where I am today, both personally and professionally, if I hadn't dared to dream of a future brighter than the one I was told I could achieve. Tap into what you truly want – no matter how big or small – and aim with intention to get there.

THE POWER OF IMAGINATION

There's a reason that some industries are primarily made up of misfits. Take the gaming industry, for example – a 2020 diversity census[2] found that a staggering twenty-one per cent of the UK industry identifies as LGBT+ in some way. Could it be that queer people are drawn to the idea of building fantasy worlds to escape from harsh reality?

Then there's the fashion industry, full of mind-bogglingly creative queer pioneers like Gareth Pugh, Alexander McQueen, Jean Paul Gaultier... the list continues, darling! These fantastical misfits stepped way outside the box and brought their wildest visions to life, reclaiming the bizarre, the grotesque and the straight-up weird to create worlds of unparalleled imagination that set them apart from other designers in an often safe, commercial industry.

It's not just queer communities, either. Afrofuturism[3] is a movement with roots in the art of Black pioneers like musician Sun Ra and sci-fi genius Octavia E. Butler, whose novels fused sheer fantasy with prescient commentaries on inequality, religion and police brutality. It's a philosophy and school of thought, which uses art and literature to confront the bloody ghosts of the colonial past and turn them into something forward-thinking, beautiful and utterly drenched in creativity. Afrofuturism was born of the power to imagine worlds kinder than the one we live in right now, and it's a vital school of thought that has inspired revolutionary misfits across the globe.

Without imagination, none of this exists.

Build Your Utopia

I recently had a lightbulb moment when I realised I'd spent a huge part of my life creating fantasy worlds. Whenever I felt shit as a kid, I retreated inside my mind to build new, imaginary realms which, in turn, made all the chaos and brashness of reality feel that little bit more bearable. It's something I still do on days when I feel overwhelmed; these little lands become like internal safe spaces where I can harness the power of being unique. It's almost like a fictional misfit hotel, with occupancy for just one!

Creatively concocting your sanctuary is not about losing your grip on reality: when the world outside overwhelms us, small acts of escapism can lighten the load, and set you on your way to realising who you are and what you really want. Keep your dreams in focus as you continue to evolve and step closer to your final form. This is time well spent.

This is an ability we all need to nurture. Whoever and wherever we are in this wild world, we can all squeeze our eyes tightly shut and conjure up personalised untamed, kaleidoscopic landscapes that can sustain us through even the toughest days. But for misfits dealing with the real-world trauma of being cast aside, such refuge becomes even more important. If existing outside the proverbial, prescriptive box is a given for misfits, then thinking outside it is not only in our nature but is our salvation.

CREATE YOUR HAPPY PLACE

What does a happy place look like to you? Perhaps, like mine, yours is a dream island, or perhaps it's a beautiful meadow filled with flowers on a summer's day, or perhaps it's a utopic music festival.

If you're struggling to think of somewhere entirely imagined, think back to treasured memories of places that have brought you joy, calm and meaning. Begin to visualise that place.

Start with the landscape – what can you see? An open sky, a boundless sea, a beautiful building? What are the textures and colours? What can you smell? Find your favourite spot in this imagined utopia. Delve deep into your mind – what excites you? Dream big – it's *your* happy place!

Perhaps you are alone in this sanctuary, enjoying its quietness and stillness. Or perhaps you have brought something or someone with you – it could be a person you know, it could be someone you idolise from a distance. What can you hear? Is your happy place full of chatter and laughter, or is it quiet and calm?

Keep filling in these gaps until you have created a space so vivid that, when you close your eyes, all your senses take you there.

Remember that you can return to this place any time that you need a moment to decompress, rebalance or destress. It's a quick and easy form of therapy that doesn't require anything other than you and your imagination, so why not try it now?

WHERE CAN YOUR DREAMS TAKE YOU?

After years of repressing myself, I started to understand myself more when I learned to love being a misfit and started embracing the parts of myself I had hidden.

This was when I allowed myself to dream of a future that I might be able to actually enjoy, not just one that I'd have to survive. No matter how unrealistic they might seem, dreams can sometimes be all that keep us going on the darkest days; a glimmer of light at the end of what can feel like the never-ending tunnel of life. We all have responsibilities and a level of day-to-day mundanity that can make chasing those dreams feel like the last, least important checkbox on a great big to-do list, but it's important to nurture your imagination and actively think about things you want.

This doesn't always have to mean thinking in extremes. Maybe it's about trying that one meal you've always been curious about, or blocking out free time to go for a long walk with no fixed destination in mind. These are all tiny, tangible dreams which can lead you forwards. Of course, it's also fun to think about the truly big-picture stuff. Maybe you're aspiring to become a world leader, or a rock-star with a never-ending supply of fabulous catsuits. On the other hand, you could just be dreaming of stability, of a peaceful, contented life surrounded by a small group of your loved ones and a whole load of nature.

For me, I knew I wanted to spend my time creating a space where I could truly thrive. I wanted to escape the day-to-day grind of my underpaid, overworked jobs, and I dreamed of bringing the fantasy worlds I had always imagined to life. Luckily for me, I've had some truly wonderful people to nurture me along the way.

FIND YOUR CHEERLEADERS

It might surprise you to know that my parents have always laughed along at my chaotic attempts to realise my true potential throughout my life – from the weekly, often pretty questionable musicals I wrote as a kid to the hilarious lip-syncs with my balls hanging out as an adult, they've always been along for the ride. Whereas they were initially concerned my weirdness would single me out, they've since seen me blossom into the glorious freak I am today – and they've never been more proud.

This isn't the case for all misfits, not by a long shot – many of us are abandoned by our families if we refuse to change or shrink elements of our character, and others never have those support structures in the first place. Outside of family structures, there are endless places to find cheerleaders – from online support groups to extended friendship circles and romantic partners, your own biggest fans might be lurking in plain sight. None of this has to require being extrovert in any way, either – especially in gaming subcultures and mental health forums, there are plenty of like-minded peers ready to not only accept but embrace and encourage your weirdness. It might not happen straight away, but when the affirmation does come, it can make all the difference.

A LETTER FROM MY PARENTS

Dear Glyn,

You've always been such a gorgeous, angelic little mummy's boy! The only person you would ever come out of your shell with was your sister, Stacey. Personality-wise, you're a mixture of us both: you had your dad's sensitivity and your mum's lack of confidence, which terrified us both when you first went to school. You were so timid that we didn't know how you'd cope.

We always knew you were a bit different, too. We thought that when you started wearing your sister's clothes and asking for tights and a doll's pram for Christmas. But all kids are different, and that's a good thing, right? Nobody is the same. We never thought you were weird; in fact, we thought you were hilarious! You always had so much imagination. Whether it was building a rocket out of teddy bears or directing your own musical retelling of Henry VIII's life, you always loved being centre stage.

Still, we never second-guessed or pre-judged you – in our eyes, that's just not what you do with your kids. We have worried about your safety, but when we saw you dressed up in drag for Sink The Pink we just said a silent prayer of thanks that your taste had improved. Baby Glyn looked like a bag lady! But as you've grown up, we've learned so much from you. It's a wonderful thing to watch your child become an adult and start going their own way. All we could ever do is be there and encourage you, and to just be glad that you're happy. It's all we've ever wanted and all we've ever asked for.

EMBRACE WHOEVER BRINGS OUT YOUR

BEST

Creating Sink The Pink has been arguably the biggest and most meaningful achievement of my life, so naturally I'll never forget the night I met Amy Zing, my wonderful co-founder and partner-in-crime – she truly was the flamboyant homosexual I had always wanted to be! Amy spoke in a series of camp pops and whistles; she was basically a walking limp wrist of sparkling emojis. We had an instant connection, the kind I had never felt with anyone else. Amy actually called herself 'the coming out service' – so many mutual friends had come to her for advice and left as the screaming, fabulous queens they were destined to become. I could feel that I was next – and boy was I ready!

From that moment on, I had the biggest cheerleader in my life. Amy saw a person in me who I was too terrified to expose and she slowly pulled it out of me, high-kicking and encouraging me along the whole way!

As Amy and I got to know each other better, all the enormous dreams of fun, fantasy and the freedom to be wholly, unapologetically myself started to come full circle. Together, we threw around ridiculous ideas for a club night and, before long, we had co-founded Sink The Pink: the most inclusive, LGBTQ+ night out in the UK. Amy saw me like nobody ever had before, and she pulled me out of my own head. Together, we were united by the belief that anything is possible. No matter how enormous the dreams I conjured up, Amy reaffirmed my belief in the power of dreaming big.

Think about who *your* cheerleader is. A cheerleader is someone who supports your dreams and wild ideas, no matter how wild they are. They believe in you more than you believe in yourself, and they give you the motivation to keep going when you're doubting everything. Your cheerleader may be immediately obvious to you or it may take some thought to identify them. They could be a friend, colleague, sibling or parent, but it's important to identify your person, so that you can turn to them when things get tough and also provide them with the same unwavering support.

PHONE A FRIEND

AMY ZING

Glyn As much as Sink The Pink is about drag, it's also about creating something bigger for people who don't feel like they have a place in the world. What do you think it is about what we've created that's drawn universal misfits to us?

Amy I think we were always just about embracing silliness, and embracing the idea of being misfits. We admired drag, but the real legacy of what we created is in the misfits, really. It's in the mini-versions of us that come into the pubs, the people who see themselves in those spaces and feel like they've found a home. These outlets are vital; they're beyond important, they're genuinely like a life force in the sense that they give us a reason to live. The term 'misfit' feels like it fits really well; we all didn't quite fit in to normal clubs.

Glyn

You really are my ultimate cheerleader – I remember the night you encouraged me to put a flick of eyeliner on, to dip my toes into self-expression. What's the power of running into who you truly are?

Amy

Well I've found my cheerleaders within Sink The Pink, too! It's about being surrounded by encouragement; it's like you're being passed a torch of responsibility. For all those years, we would kind of worship at the altars of drag, and of misfits more generally. Then, we became that for others.

Glyn

Why is it so important to you to carry that torch of inclusivity within all the work you do now?

Amy

Representing those who are under-represented really is my whole purpose. I moved to Margate to set up an LGBT youth group, launch a Pride event, to run a women's arts festival for charity. These issues of equality have been like going through therapy for me, in the sense that I know there's something really great in what we've started, yet there isn't a rulebook. To be able to create that rulebook makes me feel really lucky!

Glyn I think we've both always wanted to live in a little misfit utopia, and I feel like you've played an integral part in creating that for Margate.

Amy That's because I was super-powered by Sink The Pink. For me, the beauty of those early Sink The Pink parties – the ones where we would create events for, like, 100 people –is that we were doing them purely because we loved it. We didn't do it because there were dollar signs in our eyes, or because we wanted to be on TV. We would take a few pictures at the beginning of the night, but then nobody was taking pictures on the dance floor – so the kind of shit that would go down then wouldn't go down now, because everything is being photographed!

I'm so honoured to have been part of creating all of this, both with Sink The Pink and here in Margate. Now, I look forward to taking more of an elders' seat and creating space for new misfits to thrive.

Glyn I'm starting to feel that way too. I'm good with that – I want to be an elder, but I also want to be an icon!

Amy Definitely, I'm happy that what we've done is still going to have an impact, but I do not need to be front and centre. That's why we're such a good double act – I just like being part of a team.

Glyn Exactly. You really are the ultimate cheerleader.

✓ SET GOALS TO SUCCƎED

You know by now that you're already brimming with potential, and hopefully that realisation – as well as the understanding that the societal codes that keep us boxed in are actually a load of fictional bullshit – has encouraged you to cast off the shackles and allow yourself to really, truly think about what *you* want.

Setting these goals is the first step towards manifesting them. Think about what you want to achieve and how you're going to make it happen. Even if your dreams feel lightyears away, writing them down cements them and gives you the first and most important push.

Naturally there'll be obstacles along the way. You'll meet people who try to dim your shine to make themselves feel better, as well as a whole host of fucked-up discrimination thrown your way solely because you're a misfit. The road to living your best, most fabulous life is paved with piles of dogshit, but once you learn to side-step the naysayers and shimmy past the obstacles, you'll remain on the right track – just remember to maintain your laser focus on your wildest dreams, and on your plan for how to make them a reality.

CHAPTER 3

STICKS AND

STO

NES
NES

THE POWER OF WORDS

'Sticks and stones may break your bones, but words can never hurt you.'

Most misfits know what it's like to bullied. Therefore, we also know that this classic, endlessly repeated saying is total bullshit.

Subtle Aggressions

Whether it's your identity – race, gender, sexuality, disability – or your character – too quiet, too loud, too awkward, too eager – there's a laundry list of traits that can easily lead to bullying, and this doesn't always mean being attacked physically. It doesn't always have to be dramatic, either – we think of bullying as name-calling, pushing around and hurling slurs at strangers, but it can manifest in much more subtle ways.

Microaggressions are a key example. According to a 2015 *Vox* article[1] by Jenée Desmond-Harris, 'microaggressions are more than just insults, insensitive comments, or generalised jerky behaviour'. Instead, they're 'the kinds of remarks, questions, or actions that are painful because they have to do with a person's membership in a group that's discriminated against or subject to stereotypes,' and they often fly under the radar as they can be extremely casual and read as throwaway remarks.

Think of the way that Black women in particular are stereotyped as angry and aggressive, or the way that queer people are so often told: 'Oh, you don't *look* gay!' It could be as simple as telling someone they're 'pretty for a fat person', or praising a disabled person's intelligence in a way that's patronising or condescending. When we hear comments like these about ourselves, we're told to brush them off because the person likely didn't *mean* any harm, yet over time their impact builds and, again, proves unequivocally that words very much can hurt, even if they weren't meant to.

A Lasting Impact

There is one personal experience I will never forget. I had just come out, and I was feeling vulnerable as I'd just returned to my home city after a year in Australia. I wanted to face things head-on, so I decided I would walk into my old local pub – the place where all my old school friends and family members had been drinking for years. I had spent the previous twelve months in a total bubble, surrounded by wonderful queer people, so I was feeling brave.

The second I stepped foot in that pub, I regretted it. I felt whispers coming from the corners of the room, and then the burning, chastising stares. Finally, I heard a few faint muttered slurs.

As I sat by the bar, the noise started to settle and I started to feel a little more secure – maybe this wasn't such a bad idea after all? I began to relax, but as I did, an old bully from my past appeared and stood staring right at me. After an awkward silence, he started chanting: 'AIDS, AIDS, AIDS' in my face, getting louder and closer. I could feel my knees trembling and my voice breaking as I got up and walked to the toilet. That day will always stay with me; even as I've grown in confidence over the years, I still second-guess myself when I step into a new venue.

A Different Kind of Pain

Now, back to that old aphorism that tells us in no uncertain terms that 'words can never hurt us'. *Of course* I knew back then that a few insults couldn't crack my skull – nobody ever got wheeled off to the hospital because some stranger on the side of a road called them a wanker. But nefarious soundbites like these can warp and distort our perceptions of pain.

It's the equivalent of telling a crying, bullied child: 'Sure, someone has been calling you nasty names for years, but they *could* have bludgeoned you over the head with a rock! Think how lucky you are in comparison!' And sure, sometimes statements like these can jolt you out of your funk and remind you to look at the bigger picture. And yes, there are huge, heavy conversations to be had about perspective and privilege, which we'll get to later in this chapter.

Still, the idea that 'words can never hurt you' is a fundamental misunderstanding of the nature of pain. Physical pain is familiar to us all, and often manifests quite literally and visibly. Emotional pain can be a lot harder to notice and label or confidently express, but the power of words is undeniable. When everyone around you is telling you to 'step back', 'be the bigger person' and let insults 'wash over you' like 'water off a duck's back', you question yourself. Statements like these can trick us into thinking that the very, very real emotional pain we're feeling is either a figment of our imaginations or a failing on our part.

Words might not inflict the same sharp shock of agony as a twisted leg; instead, it might be the knot in your stomach that twists and gnarls as you step out onto the street. Perhaps it's that dull, throbbing ache that persists as you try to drag yourself through yet another day of being stared at, insulted and made to feel worthless. It can even be an all-encompassing, internal flatline that makes dragging your weary limbs out of bed feel like running a marathon. These are all extremely real, internal variants of pain, and they can all be snapped into action with appalling ease through a mere handful of thoughtless or harmful words.

A LETTER TO MY BULLIES

Writing can be a catharsis when you are feeling overwhelmed.

This has been used to great effect by Jade Thirlwall, one-third of the astronomically successful girl band Little Mix. Before the fame and fortune, Jade was a self-described 'shy, nerdy, quiet' girl growing up in a working-class family in the British coastal town of South Shields. 'For Christmas I would ask for a Shakespeare book instead of a Barbie, so people would rip the piss out of me,' she laughs from her bedroom, ever the down-to-earth megastar as she adjusts her bright blue under-eye mask.

Even with global stardom, the bullies are still ever-looming – but now, they manifest in the form of online trolls and awful gossip website comment sections filled with catty remarks. There's also Jade's never-ending struggle of navigating high-pressure meetings, and fighting to have her voice heard and taken seriously: 'You're sat there in a meeting trying to tell them that your opinion is just as important as theirs, but it's difficult when you're from two different worlds.' Despite these ongoing battles, Jade has learned to conquer her bullies and carve out success on her own terms.

On the next page, she shares a letter to her bullies – once you've had a read, try writing a letter for yourself and see how it makes you feel.

A LETTER FROM JADE THIRLWALL

When I was young, I never knew where I fit in. I still don't know now which boxes I tick: I don't conform to the normal gender ideals of what a woman should be, and I guess being mixed-race, I was never Black enough to be in the Black community, never white enough to be white, never Arab enough to be in that community.

Bullies, you saw that. You bullied me badly throughout my childhood and teenage years, and because of that, I've always been kind of a nervous wreck. When I was around thirteen years old, I developed an eating disorder. When everything else was out of control, anorexia was a way of feeling like I had something I could control myself.

I thought I had escaped the bullies when I left school. I entered this superstar world and thought it would stop, but no Hun! If anything, it's the opposite – now I've got even more scrutiny and judgement, constantly. Our culture almost celebrates bullying – just look at the comments sections. But as I got older, I learned to use your insults as fuel. 'You don't think I can do this? I'll prove you wrong!'

Although I still don't quite know where I fit in, I've learned to not need answers to those questions. The moment I realised I didn't need a term for who or what I am, I felt more free. Now I've learned not to listen to the self-saboteur in my head, the one that loops all of your horrible words in my mind. If I'm feeling a bit shit, I know that the more I tell myself positive things, the more it all goes in.

Even better, now I get to stand onstage and see mini-mes in the crowd. It warms my heart when I see happy gay couples, or a trans fan with a sign saying, 'You've helped me'. I get to use my platform to influence others now; I get to be that role model to help fans overcome their bullies. There really is no better feeling than that.

'I was never Black enough to be in the Black community, never white enough to be white, never Arab enough to be in that community.'

M∃NTAL HEALTH MATTᴇᴙS

Life can be difficult enough without the 'misfit' label
to contend with, so it's no surprise that marginalised
people across the board suffer disproportionate rates
of poor mental health. First of all, there's bullying – a
common thread linking misfit experiences worldwide.
A 2017 study published in the *Journal of Child Psychology
and Psychiatry*[2] found that childhood bullying contributes
to long-term mental health problems, which can persist
up to midlife.

The internet might have given us endless cute animal memes and
the opportunity to connect with like-minded misfits worldwide, but
it's also created a shitty new phenomenon of its own: cyberbullying.
Statistics released in 2019 by the Cyberbullying Research Center[3]
found thirty-seven per cent of the almost five thousand twelve- to
seventeen-year-olds in the study in the US had experienced repeated,
targeted online harassment at least once in their lifetime, with teenage
girls more likely to suffer this online abuse.

Identity plays a huge part when it comes to mental health too. In a 2019
report, the Race Equality Foundation[4] found that not only are people of
colour in the UK 'at high risk of mental ill health and disproportionately
impacted by social detriments associated with mental illness' (such as
racism and income inequality), they're also more likely to report 'harsh
experiences' when seeking help and treatment.

Statistics published in 2018 by leading UK LGBTQ+ charity Stonewall[5]
similarly found that fifty-two per cent of five thousand respondents
had experienced depression in the last year; thirteen per cent had
attempted suicide. Trans, non-binary and gender non-conforming
communities also reported disproportionately high rates of suicidal
ideation, self-harm and addiction, whereas charities like the Albert

Kennedy Trust (AKT) also highlight that young queer people are disproportionately vulnerable to homelessness after coming out to their families.

Mental health conditions are also exacerbated by a wider lack of understanding. Many of us deal with conditions like anxiety, depression, obsessive-compulsive disorder (OCD) and bipolar disorder, yet they're still too often stigmatised or not picked up on by healthcare professionals. The same can be said for neurodiversity. We're too often told there's such a thing as a 'normal' brain, but there's a growing understanding that conditions like autism and ADHD (attention deficit hyperactivity disorder) aren't inherently negative; they're simply proof of the fact that not all brains function in the same way.

Naming specificities can open up a whole world of information and shared experience, as well as handy tips to understand how your unique brain works. It could be as simple as needing clearer cues for communication, or a realisation that certain situations send our stress levels sky-rocketing. Whatever your brain needs to keep ticking along, knowledge is power – and if society wasn't so relentlessly judgemental when it comes to mental health across the board, we'd feel a lot less worried about unpicking the complexities of our own innermost thoughts and feelings.

In an ideal world, we'd all be able to access stigma-free, judgement-free help to navigate the real-life mental health consequences of living as a misfit, but mental health services are low on government funding priority lists across the world, with waiting lists stretching for months, sometimes years. As a result, community-led NGOs are forced to step in and provide vital services. If you're struggling yourself there's a list of resources at the end of this book (see pages 168–70).

ACKNOWLEDGE YOUR PAIN

Dealing with mental demons is always a difficult, isolating process, but it's one that's endlessly exacerbated by the stigma that still comes with speaking openly about mental illness.

You may have experienced days when getting out of bed feels like too much of a mountain to climb, and on these days, switching off and locking yourself away can feel like the most tempting response. Instead, remember that there's something truly life-changing about learning to voice your pain. From accessing online therapy services to seeking the comfort of a trusted shoulder to cry on, there's no shame in speaking openly about your struggles.

You Are Not Alone

Especially in today's warped world of social media, it's easier than ever to trick yourself into believing that life is all sunshine and rainbows, particularly for non-misfits. You might get jealous and envy their lot. But when you're thinking clearly and logically, you will recall that everyone, no matter who they are, faces pain at some point in their lives. This pain is extremely real to them and isn't something you can directly compare to or measure against your own.

Yet when hurtful words are thrown at you, you won't be thinking clearly and logically. In real time, your beautiful mind will melt into a scary, messy puddle that shakes those healthy, mental foundations that you desperately need to survive in this world, and sometimes those repercussions last for years.

In those moments of internal chaos, you can get so overwhelmed by your own pain that you forget that others experience it too. You convince yourself that everyone else can just get back up when they're knocked down, whether physically or mentally. You tell yourself that everyone else is able to just let it wash over them and get on with it – so why can't you? When trauma strips the perspective, you need to remember that your pain will pass, but your mind tumbles easily into steep downward spirals.

At this point, your mind cranks into overdrive. You misconstrue pain for weakness, and then you become embarrassed by those thoughts. Instead of acknowledging them, you minimise them. You brush them off, dial them down, bottle them up. Maybe you are worried about judgement, or that someone will misunderstand all the curious quirks that make you a misfit. In those moments, reaching out can feel like a risk. Mentally, it can feel like you're opening yourself up to the possibility of yet more words that cause pain. Not words of anger, but words of misunderstanding.

Coping Mechanisms

Allowing yourself to be vulnerable, however, is the greatest gift you can give yourself. Seek help, even medication if you need it – and in the meantime, try to find coping mechanisms to weather the worst of the storm while you seek longer-term help. Whether it's meditation, journalling or just a long walk, find methods of acknowledging and then processing your anger, pain and sadness. Don't run away from your thoughts: sit, digest, acknowledge and share them. Give yourself permission to speak out loud to nobody in particular.

Whenever I feel particularly shit, I like to go through this process of voicing my feelings and then letting them just linger. Like me, you can think of it as a chrysalis of sorrow: identify those emotions, spit them out in front of you and then let them envelop you. Don't buy into the myth that you're 'wallowing' in sorrow, and don't submit to the glossy, overly optimistic attitude that tells us to swipe away our pain rather than acknowledging it.

Don't let any fucker repeat the old 'sticks and stones' chant. No! Instead, build that chrysalis and let yourself slide inside its walls. Give yourself time to really sit with those emotions, and understand that acknowledging them is part of the process we all need to go through to truly evolve into fully-fledged, beautiful new beasts.

Allowing yourself to be vulnerable is the greatest gift you can give yourself.

FIND YOUR

CATHARSIS

In the opening episode of the television series *The Bold Type*, three young women stand on a busy subway platform and scream at the top of their lungs. It's a common trope, really – think back to Björk's mega-hit 'Hyperballad', where the Icelandic megastar sings about waking up at the top of a mountain and throwing shit off the top just to feel something. Relatable, right?

In an ideal world, everyone would have access to their own secluded mountain or rooms filled with stuff to smash when the world gets too much, maybe even a giant, inflatable house to throw yourself into and thrash out your rage. We're often told to suppress our anger, but rarely does anyone stop to think where that anger might have come from. Misfits know only too well the fury that can bubble up under the surface, especially when you're moving through a world that makes you feel like you have no place within it.

Finding outlets to express these feelings is essential. One only needs to glance at many news headlines to see the chaos that reigns when fury is left to fester. Maybe you're someone that likes to pound the streets with heavy metal blaring through your headphones, or perhaps you prefer an intense workout.

Personally, I've found that manifestation and affirmations help me most. Whenever someone tells me I can't do something, I silence that noise and believe I can, and it's their doubt that makes me strive twice as hard to make it happen, partly as a 'Fuck You!'. It might sound cheesy, but giving yourself a pep talk can be just the ticket you need to get through a shitty day. Telling yourself that you're strong, brave and powerful, and then accepting it is often half the battle – so speak to yourself and say what you need to hear right now. I also make sure to be the biggest cheerleader possible for those around me – it starts a chain of positivity that feels infectious, and brings me closer to others who might struggle to acknowledge and accept their own worth, too.

When all else fails, I push myself to erupt into cackling, hysterical laughter – my poor neighbours! Whether I'm laughing at life, myself or some shade of ridiculousness I've seen somewhere, I've always found that laughter is the best fuel; even if I have to force it, pushing those chuckles out always helps me find the lightness in life. Next time you're feeling low, try spending more time with the funniest people in your life or watch something you find really hilarious online. Laughter can be an amazing form of therapy, and it can really help you process the anger by letting it come to the surface instead of suppressing it.

Humour Can Be Healing

Some of the most hilarious people I know are the ones who have had to overcome the most obstacles. As an industry, stand-up comedy sometimes gets a bad rep – and sure, there are still way too many white, straight, cis male comedians who seize any opportunity to punch down at marginalised communities with bad-faith jokes. Yet there have also long been a number of brilliant comedians – think Gina Yashere, Hannah Gadsby, even Alan Carr – using their time onstage to take the piss out of the world and serve up some serious home truths along the way.

Among these, Rosie Jones is exemplary. You might have seen her cracking jokes on television, but if you haven't, just know that she's a hilarious, take-no-prisoners superstar with a sarcastic sense of humour and a personality that's impossible not to fall in love with. A self-described misfit with an arsenal of side-splitting one-liners at her disposal, Rosie has always known how to use humour to stick two fingers up at bullies and truly claim her self-confidence.

ROSIE JONES DOESN'T GIVE A FUCK

I've got cerebral palsy, so I've been disabled since birth. I was famous before I was famous because coming from a little seaside town, I was the disabled one. 'Oh, who's that wobbling down the street? It's Rosie!'

I've always been called a misfit because I stood out, but I never remember feeling sad or wanting to be able-bodied. I need to acknowledge that some people are mercilessly bullied, and it's horrible. But what I heard at school was: 'Rosie, you walk funny!' I would say: 'I do, you make a good point!' My mum always said that I literally could not be bullied, because any comment anyone made, I just agreed with it!

I probably didn't embrace my other misfit qualities though; I thought being disabled *and* a geek and into comic books and dressing too brightly would be too much. From the age of four years old, I knew I wanted to kiss girls too; I watched *Superman* and wanted to kiss Lois Lane. Because there was no disabled queer representation, it took me until I was twenty-five years old to figure out who I was. It's been a long journey, so now I embrace every single aspect of myself: I'm loud, I'm annoying, I'm goofy, I'm disabled and I'm gay, and I'll never apologise for being me.

Despite that, there's still this archaic notion that we need to fit into society. In reality, society is weird, wonderful and made up of so many beautifully diverse people. Society moves *with* the people, so I don't think anyone should fit in. Be yourself – and if anyone says you're 'too much', just know that's absolute bullshit, because these are the qualities that make you *you*. Be proud of them.

PRIVILEGE & STRUGGLES

In a world obsessed with simplistic narratives, it's easy to forget that multiple things can be true at the same time, and that none of them cancel each other out. Your pain is legitimate. It needs to be acknowledged, processed and worked through in your own time. On the other hand, it will also always be true that you are not alone in feeling pain and that your struggles can easily pale in comparison to what other people are going through across the world.

Being reminded of this fact while you're suffering doesn't feel helpful, right? If anything, when your own brain is drowned and overwhelmed, it makes you feel worse – like you're a shitty or selfish person for losing sight of the bigger picture. This is when we get defensive. We lash out.

Timing and context are everything. When someone else's pain is used as a weapon to minimise your own, it's frustrating. Despite this, being reminded of your place in the wider world is essential. So when you have managed to work your way through that cycle, it's important to zoom out and think seriously about where your story and your struggles fit in on a wider, global scale.

Most of us misfits know exactly what it's like to feel excluded, especially for reasons we can't control. It's exactly this mentality – of cliques, in-groups and the bizarre myth that there's any such thing as 'normal' – that trains us to see difference first and foremost, which is totally unhelpful. To understand how this impacts collective thought, think of the difference between sympathy and empathy. When we feel sympathy, we feel pity. It's like we see someone else's struggle from a distance, and that triggers sadness but not much else. Empathy goes a step further. It's about relating to those people and their feelings. In a nutshell, it's about putting yourself in their shoes.

Some of us bristle at words like 'privilege'. There's this idea that acknowledging your privilege means that your story is minimised, and that you've been popped through a machine that flattens your identity, your character, your life, into a series of boxes. This isn't the case, at all. If you're white, you will not be impacted by racism. If you're straight, you won't be impacted by homophobia. If you're cisgender, you won't feel the brunt of transphobia. These are just facts. Thinking about identity in this way isn't reductive, no matter what anyone might argue.

It's not diminishing your struggle to acknowledge that you've had an easier life than other people, nor is it overly simplistic to say that we all fall somewhere on a worldwide scale of privilege based on everything from bodies and gender to size and skin colour.

DISSƎCTING A_LLYSHIP

It sometimes feels like the word 'ally' is everywhere. But what does it actually mean? In a nutshell, 'allyship' means understanding your privilege and then leveraging it to help out other, more marginalised people. It means standing by the side of those who need your support, and sometimes taking risks where they might not be able to.

Here, context is key. Especially as so much of our modern-day activism plays out online, this allyship can be performative at best and straight-up harmful at worst. When George Floyd was murdered by police officer Derek Chauvin in 2020, well-meaning white people began posting black squares to their grid with the hashtag #BlackoutTuesday or #BlackLivesMatter. All this did was fill the #BlackLivesMatter feed with black squares, making information about donations, protest safety tactics and demonstration locations difficult to find.[6]

The reality is that when it comes to fighting discrimination that disproportionately fucks over misfits of all descriptions, there is no easy way to be an ally.

What Can You Do?

The first, most important lesson is to know when to listen. This isn't about you or your ego, and it's not about looking good online. Allyship means knowing when to take a step back, and when to, for example, create platforms for marginalised groups to speak about their lived experiences. It's about understanding that, on some subjects, you'll never be an authority. If you're white, you can read as much anti-racist theory as you like. All the books in the world will never give you the right to snatch the microphone away from a person of colour, but what you can do is amplify voices when they're being silenced and share resources when they're needed.

'Seek out the stories of people who don't look like you, and absorb them with an open mind.'

The first, most important lesson is to know when to listen.

Maybe you're financially stable – how could you redistribute that extra wealth to people who might need it more urgently? This doesn't always mean money, either. It can be as simple as volunteering or advocating for people who don't get opportunities when you do.

The next thing to remember is that allyship is a journey, not a destination. You *will* fuck up. We're all born and raised in a world built on bigotry, judgement and oppression, no matter where in the world we are. Whether we like it or not, we'll all internalise discriminatory beliefs at some point. The challenge is to recognise them, name them and then learn how to move past them. Sometimes, you won't do this perfectly. If that is the case, be open to being called out. Don't take it personally. Apologise, make a mental note and then move on.

Reading won't solve everything, but representation and visibility are key to understanding not only our differences, but our commonalities too. Seek out the stories of people who don't look like you, and absorb them with an open mind. Before long, the differences will begin to seep away and you'll start to understand that your humanity links you to everyone, no matter their walk of life. When you get to that point of seeing yourself in others who don't share your struggles, the process of moving from sympathy to empathy is a lot easier.

When someone more marginalised than you is being oppressed, try to relate to them on this emotional, personal level. We all live under global structures of capitalism and imperialism, and we misfits fall victim to the kind of old-fashioned, discriminatory thinking that keeps us all down. Understanding your differences and acknowledging your privileges are key steps on the road towards actually living by a motto of allyship, but realising that so many of us are being fucked over by the same systems can lead to the kind of genuine solidarity that makes bigots quake in their boots.

Ultimately, there's real strength in sharing your experiences and learning from people from all different walks of life. You'll always find shreds of commonality to hold onto; not only will they make your own struggles feel less isolating, these vital stories will help you understand that fighting your own demons gets easier when you're battling with other misfits to get rid of horrible, bullshit discrimination across the board.

CHAPTER 4

CHASE
YOUR

JOY

WHAT MAKES YOU HAPPY?

It's one of the world's most frequently asked questions, and it ties into big, existential issues, the kind of burning hot topics that have kept scientists, academics and philosophers occupied and confused as hell for centuries. On a basic level, as already discussed in Chapter Two (see page 38), there's a kind of expected trajectory that we're supposed to tick off as we move through life – education, career, marriage, kids.

Remember when I said earlier that we misfits can't adhere to these rules? It remains true, but that might not be such a bad thing.

We're constantly sold the idea that working towards goals is the only way to achieve fulfilment; capitalism tells us that the more productive we are, the happier we'll be. Leading academic Dr Tal Ben-Shahar called bullshit on this when he coined the term 'arrival fallacy'.[1] On paper, he had it all – endless academics praising his work, a fancy title and even a global reputation as an elite squash player.

When gearing up for a new squash tournament, he convinced himself that victory would ultimately make him feel fulfilled, truly happy. He won, and felt a short jolt of joy. But that dissipated quickly, and then the stress, pressure and lack of fulfilment returned. Ben-Shahar used this experience to flesh out the wider theory of an 'arrival fallacy', which describes the false promise of happiness linked to setting goals and achieving them. Ultimately, on the endless treadmill of conservatism and capitalism, this is what we're all taught to do: aim for the job, the promotion, the white picket fence and the security. Yet even non-misfits are starting to realise that following these generic, heteronormative ideals doesn't quite work.

Make Your Own Blueprint

We've already acknowledged just how much extra bullshit we misfits have to wade through in order to truly appreciate ourselves as the resilient, unique weirdos we truly are, but there's plenty of joy to be found when you embrace everything that makes you different.

Think about the idea of the arrival fallacy, and how much we all strive towards arbitrary goals that are presented to us by the world. For me, marriage was never on the cards because it was literally illegal for me to marry someone I actually loved. Luckily, activists fighting for marriage equality have continued to make crucial gains for LGBTQ+ people worldwide, but from a young age I was forced to question these key institutions because, at one point, it looked like they would never accept me, or other misfits like me.

As societies worldwide continue to question the idea of 'normality', as well as who established the idea and why, we're coming up

It's about casting off the external forces and tuning in to whatever does make you happy.

with forward-thinking blueprints for building happiness on our own terms. Think about communal living, queer families and polyamorous relationships as just a few examples – generally speaking, it's the misfits driving these interrogations of what happiness could look like.

For many who don't see themselves in ads or even in media more generally, lack of representation also helps to dispel the capitalist myth that true happiness is linked to buying shit. So no, happiness isn't about success, or weight loss, or that magic new gadget that's sold as an absolute must-have. Instead, it's about understanding that what we're told – that we need the perfect car, house, haircut or romantic partner – is being said to us for a reason, and usually that reason involves us parting with our hard-earned cash or striving for impossible goals. Happiness isn't about thinking: 'Oh fuck, I'll *never* be married by 30.' Instead, it's about thinking: 'Well, who the hell says I have to do that anyway?' It's about casting off the expectations of your society, your culture, the external forces feeding you the kind of subconscious blueprints for life that keep you awake at night, and tuning in to whatever does make you happy.

Generally speaking, most societies don't want you to do this. Multi-million-pound industries, such as the wellness, diet and beauty industries, are built on the premise that right now you're not good enough, but if you buy all of their shit, you'll get there. You'll reach that impossible pinnacle of self-fulfilment, which will, in turn, bring you joy. It's a process that begins when you're still young, impressionable and filling in the first few chapters of your own story.

That's why truly understanding your own parameters of joy and building your life around those values is a radical act in and of itself. You're opting to ignore the messages being fed to you, paving your own way and building your own future, baby! Your imagination can truly run wild if you let go of whatever you're being *told* can make you happy and start thinking about what *actually* makes you happy.

Maybe you don't *want* the kids, the marriage, the huge house in the countryside. It could be that all those self-care tips – meditation, journalling, hot baths – just don't bring you pleasure, and all you really want is to play your favourite video game or thrash out your frustrations to your favourite music. The minute you start drilling down to figure out where your happiness truly lies, you'll find yourself staring face-to-face with life's biggest questions without a gnawing sense of pressure. Now, you've reached the great unlearning.

IN PURSUIT OF COLOUR

As a fellow fabulous drag weirdo complete with facial hair, I see a lot of myself in Gilbert Baker, creator of the iconic rainbow Pride flag, which now hangs on all sorts of buildings and crops up at protests worldwide.

After years spent serving in the military, he settled in San Francisco to be surrounded by beautiful, queer misfits and eventually ended up becoming close friends with Harvey Milk, a trailblazing politician and queer activist. Frustrated by the fact that the LGBTQ+ community didn't then have any kind of joyous, uplifting symbol – the only real symbol we had was the pink triangle, which was printed onto the uniforms of gay concentration camp prisoners in Nazi Germany – Milk tasked Baker with creating one ahead of San Francisco's Freedom Day Parade in 1978.

Depending on who you ask, the resulting rainbow design was inspired by the American flag (he saw the power of the flag as a symbol after America's bicentennial), the colourful nature of the LGBTQ+ community or Judy Garland's camp classic 'Over the Rainbow'.

The original design had eight stripes, each with a meaning: pink for sexuality, red for life, orange for healing, yellow for sunlight, green for nature, turquoise for art and magic, indigo for serenity and violet for spirit. I've always been inspired by Baker – like the radical drag trailblazer, I ran headfirst into colour with my balls hanging out of my leotard, using paint, costumes and ridiculous performances as a vehicle to launch myself headlong into the pursuit of joy.

FANCY A SLICE?

Someone else that embodies the ethos of using camp, colour and chaos to channel the joy of queerness is Ginny Lemon, a drag artist who shook up *RuPaul's Drag Race UK* with a pair of canary-yellow Crocs, a cheeky smile and that infectious catchphrase: 'Fancy a slice?'

Ginny might drip with charisma now, but the drag genius – think technicolour Kate Bush on acid – hasn't always been so radiant. In fact, Lewis – who uses they/them pronouns out of drag – dreamed up Ginny as an effervescent vehicle to work through the emotional fall-out of two family deaths – Lewis's older brother, in 2011, and then their sister, Emma, in 2016.

Colour played a huge part in this transformation. You know that old saying, 'dress for the mood you want'? There *is* some truth to it – for Ginny at least, leaning into the boldest, most beautiful hues of life enabled a new, fabulous creature to take shape. 'Drag was my way of escaping grief and channelling all of that negative energy into something, hence the colour yellow,' they tell me via Zoom, their make-up a glorious riot of dark red lippy, emerald blue eyeshadow and, of course, neon yellow brows. 'Not only is yellow the non-binary colour, it's also one of spiritual healing. I surrounded myself with that, as protection from what was going on. I guess you could say I paved my own yellow brick road!'

You can do this too – but your vehicle doesn't have to be drag. Maybe you want to pour all of your inner workings-out into a journal, or perhaps there's even a sport you could throw yourself into to gain confidence and feel emboldened to explore different aspects of yourself. It might be as easy as experimenting with make-up tricks on a daily basis, or adding a sprinkle of glitz into your wardrobe. Whatever it is, the key is to embrace the most beautifully bizarre parts of yourself that normally get stamped deep down, and find a way to channel that colourful chaos – it could be a full ballgown or something as simple as a painted nail or tie-dye top if you prefer to be dialled-down – into something creative.

Even after becoming one of the UK's weirdest, most wonderful drag superstars, Lewis still needs semi-regular reminders to chase the joy of colour in their everyday life – so if you feel yourself forgetting to truly embrace the kaleidoscope of life, know you're not alone. To add a pep to your step, there's nothing like self-expression to pull you out of an emotional rut. For Lewis, this realisation came during a spring clean. 'I actually cleared out my wardrobe recently,' they recall. 'I literally dressed like an indecisive bee – either yellow or dressed in black, mourning for my life!' Their husband walked in on this sartorial detox and asked: 'Do you really need seven plain, black, large T-shirts? Don't you think your big, black and baggy days are over?'

This subtle read sparked a few epiphanies we could all learn a little from: spring-cleaning is good for the soul, dressing for the mood you want *can* actually work and considering how you want to express yourself to the world can be an integral part of stepping into your truest self. 'I sat up late and ordered myself a whole bunch of colour,' Ginny laughs, before leaving on a quintessentially Ginny note: 'The world is a rainbow, and I want to taste it, baby!'

'THE WORLD IS A RAINBOW, AND I WANT TO TASTE IT, BABY!'

UNLEARN
THE ART
OF
SELF-SABOTAGE

Back in 2016, a wise woman named Marie Kondo popped up on Netflix with a rule that struck a chord with audiences worldwide: get rid of anything in your life that doesn't spark joy. Backed by a film crew and decades of expertise as a best-selling author and cleaning guru, she travelled to the homes of hoarders and stripped back the clutter. Most importantly, she delved deep into the lives of these chaotic collectors to peel back the layers of the life stories, and then asked them to look beyond themselves and simply spend a moment of silence contemplating how the things in their life made them feel.

Whether we know it or not, we're all the best authors of our own stories. Each of us knows exactly what's happened in our lives and how every single one of those events has impacted us. Your mind, your routine, your personality: it's all a gigantic puzzle made up of the good, bad and the truly ugly stuff that's happened to you in the past, but it can be easy to become passengers rather than steering the ship, which is when we become susceptible to the relentless messaging telling us that we can tap into our joy by following certain rules. Plenty of us are so busy going through the day-to-day process of merely surviving that we don't stop to ask ourselves key questions, or give ourselves the space to understand how certain parts of our lives make us feel.

What Kondo did for these families was about so much more than just chucking away a few zebra-print dresses and moth-eaten pants. As well as sharing her wisdom and her truly amazing folding tips (who knew the edges of a jumper could look so neat?), she gave these families of lost, confused hoarders permission to step back and really think about what makes them happy. By giving them the time and space to tackle these big-picture questions, as well as a handful of new ways to think about their lives, Kondo transformed herself into the fairy godmother of joy by zapping away the bullshit of everyday life, even if just for a second.

Filtering Out the Noise

I'm not saying you should start sifting through your wardrobe and agonising over those worn-out leggings you *swear* you'll wear again, but more that understanding what truly sparks joy requires a kind of mental blankness, a clarity that helps you see things differently. Sounds easy, right?

Well, of course not! Especially in today's world, life feels more full of noise than ever before. Even if you switch off social media, just by leaving the house you can find yourself being bombarded by messages on billboards advertising yet more shit you don't want or need. Turn on the TV? Here's a happy couple with a brand new sports car and two newly landed promotions to make you feel inadequate! We've always been fed these over-simplified, universal messages that shape our views of what 'joy' means, which might not apply in even the tiniest way to our own lives. But they're easy to internalise, especially now that they're being disseminated through more outlets than ever.

Recent statistics[2] show that more than 53 per cent of the world's population is on social media. If there are nearly eight billion people in the world, that means a whole lot of memes, selfies and inspirational quotes to dig into! Especially in countries with struggling economies, the internet has been sold as the great equaliser of the twenty-first century, a chance for more of us to learn new skills and tap into reserves of ability that we never knew we had. Thanks to a growing number of people with coding skills, grassroots organisations and talented teachers, this is often true – there are obvious, undeniable benefits to internet access for those of us lucky enough to have it. But what's the downside?

Well, comparison is the big one. In the past, you could happily trot through your own life and make your own decisions without really being aware of what anyone else was doing. You could talk to people close to you about their lives, their decisions and their problems, but ultimately you had a pretty limited view of what people were doing on a day-to-day basis. This isn't the case anymore. It takes only ten minutes on social media to see that someone on the other side of the world just took a flame emoji beach selfie, and that their best friend just bought a house with their boyfriend. Because we're still too often embarrassed by failure, we keep the truly bad shit to ourselves and curate the best bits, and while that makes us feel good, it can make other people feel pretty shitty about their lot.

A New Lens

This is especially true if you're a misfit of any description. When it feels like the world is driven by success and popularity, it can feel even harder to carve out your own lane, never mind to tune out the noise that clouds your brain when you're asking yourself that one simple yet seemingly impossible question: what makes me happy? Not only do we have a warped, distorted and heavily filtered view of everybody else's reality, we have even more examples of 'happiness' to hold up and compare to our own realities, which are bound to look pretty shit in comparison.

It might feel tricky to celebrate and own your originality when others have used it against you, but only by understanding what makes you unique can you start to view your life through a new lens. Imagine Marie Kondo stomping into your bathroom while you scroll through Instagram on the toilet. Picture her snatching your phone out of your hand, smashing it on the floor and demanding you stop comparing yourself to other people. It's only with those nudges and those reminders that we can jolt ourselves out of those habits, the ones that are truly blocking our blessings and leading us into these mindless traps of consumption, comparison and constant questioning, instead of productive, fulfilling lines of questioning. Instead of asking what have others got that you haven't, ask yourself what you're grateful for and lean into that. It's easy to lose sight of these small things with all the chaos whirling around us, but you deserve to take that time to zoom out and get a bird's-eye view of your own life. It's what Marie would want.

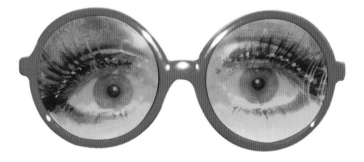

rUNinTO FEAR

Sometimes, fear is an instinctual response to danger –
if you're being chased by a grizzly bear, fear gives you
the adrenaline to run! Yet sometimes fear can be a kind
of self-sabotage instead. It can leave you too afraid of
being embarrassed or failing to chase your dreams, and
it can prevent you from making necessary but scary
steps forward on your journey towards unlocking your
superpowers as a misfit.

Growing up as a Black, gay woman in Brixton, London taught Skin, the
powerhouse rockstar lead vocalist of legendary 1990s band Skunk
Anansie, how to deal with fear. 'I'm not scared of being scared any
more,' she explains via video call from her home in Ibiza. 'Instead of
seeing things to be afraid of, I see problems that need to be fixed.
That comes from my life experiences. For example, my first boyfriend
was much older than me and really violent, so getting out of that
relationship was a matter of survival. After I got out of that situation,
I felt like I could do anything.'

But of course, not even Skin – a punk icon with an OBE to her name –
can do *everything*. 'I obviously can't,' she laughs. 'There are things I've
failed at, but I'll always give them a try. That's the key difference.'

For misfits worldwide, Skin offers some sage advice: question
your fears. 'It's about recognising the fear rather than just saying
no to a person or a situation,' she continues. 'Ask yourself – what
about this is making you scared? Is it objectively a fucking foolish
situation which you shouldn't get into and which will totally waste
your time, or are you tempted to say no because you're scared of
embarrassment or sullying your reputation?' If the answer is the

latter, it's likely your fear stems from pride rather than genuine danger – and in these cases, it's often best to get your hands dirty, no matter what happens.

Skin's closely-shaven head might be her signature look now, but finding the courage to shave all her hair off represented confronting fear, especially as a young Black woman in the early 1990s. 'It was seen as a very strange thing to do,' she says, recalling an experience where she modelled at an Afro Hair & Beauty show and found herself constantly offered free treatments by concerned stall-holders. 'I only realised afterwards that they were offering free products because they thought something was wrong with my hair; they thought I must have shaved it off because something went wrong!' Yet for Skin, it was an act of defiance.

'There's a lot of societal concern around what Black women choose to do with their hair,' says Skin, alluding to its political importance, which is well-documented in books like Emma Dabiri's *Don't Touch My Hair* and even songs like Solange's powerful song of the same name. 'Before I shaved it, I tried a curly perm and I tried straight hair,' Skin continues. 'They were examples of me going along with what society thinks I should look like, and I got fucking tired of it all – the chemicals, the mess, the amount of time and money my hair took up. Shaving it all off was the most defiant, non-conformist thing I could do, and it definitely made me have to defend myself – from my family, even from strangers on the street. Yet at the same time, it represented me grabbing hold of my own image, style and personality. It freed me from the shackles of what I was expected to look like as a Black girl.'

A WEEK OF BOLDNESS

After talking with Skin, I started thinking about fear. All of the best things in my life have happened when I've run into things I'm scared of. So now, I want you to really think about this.

What are you scared of? Is there a conversation you've been putting off? Maybe you're terrified of starting a new exercise class, or following Skin's lead and taking the plunge with a bold new haircut? Fear can be debilitating, so I want you to arrange one full week of running headfirst into it.

This might sound terrifying, so start by making a list of seven things you're afraid of. They can be big or small, as long as they're things you want to change but are currently afraid to.

Now, reorder them from the least scary to the most scary. We aren't talking about jumping out of a plane here (yet!). Maybe day one is something as simple as trying a new food you've always been apprehensive about, then day seven could even be applying for your dream job! It's totally up to you how far you take this, but diving in at the deep end is a great habit to practise.

At the end of each day, write down how far you got with that day's task and, most importantly, how confronting it made you feel. Don't punish yourself if you miss any; these can be carried forward to other days if anything seems just a little too overwhelming.

I know first-hand how daunting this can all seem – trust me, I've been that terrified person! Yet step by step, as you bash through your list, you'll start changing how you interact with fear. Soon, that familiar tingling in your stomach will start to feel like something you welcome.

You'll start to realise that with fear comes adrenaline – and who knows, you might even decide to chase it on your own!

LƎAN INTO YOUR NIᴄHE

Happiness, in my eternally chaotic life, is finally being able to snatch moments of peace. I have grappled with being an introverted extrovert all my life. Because I spent so much of my early life locked away with my own thoughts, the extrovert in me never got a chance.

Now, I can't be settled in my skin when one outshines the other, so I'm at a point in my life where I need to feed both sides of myself. I may appear to be as high-energy as a tap-dancing parrot, but when I'm not showing off, I like to do absolutely nothing. I'm truly at my happiest when I'm surrounded by loved ones and the ultimate love of my life, my dog Peanut. I can sit and talk to her for hours about what outfits she's going to wear, and about which of her fellow, shady neighbourhood bitches have been giving her the side-eye.

Other than that, happiness in my shiny, misfit life comes from indulging my tiny, peculiar obsessions. Believe it or not, I'm an avid twitcher – I feel at total peace watching birds. Rainbow lorikeets, Eurasian jays, herons, even the simple mallard duck... I could talk bird facts for days: did you know, for example, that the mallard duck has a fake womb, so it controls when it gets pregnant? Of course, there's so much else that brings me joy: slow dancing to power ballads (seriously, why doesn't that happen anymore? It feels so great!), wearing statement hats – even if I don't wear them anywhere – and spending time with my family, whether that be my chosen family, my biological family or my extended queer community.

You might feel at your happiest indulging your niche interests, for example watching films by a director none of your friends have heard of or listening to an unsigned band that no one knows. Whatever it is, make time for it and enjoy it.

Glyn There are few people in the world more valuable to me than Jay Barry Matthews, a gay fairy godmother and kindred misfit spirit whose creativity, determination and drive never fails to spark a fire under my arse! So who better to speak about the sheer euphoria of unbridled creativity?

Jay I was born an alien. I just never fit in. I came out of the womb with a broken heart in some way, feeling lost. I gravitated towards the weirdo kids. I used to play games like 'tipping out': looking in my mum's make-up drawer with all her jewellery too, tipping it out, analysing it, then putting it all back in perfectly so nobody would ever know.

Glyn Tell me about where you were in your life when we first met.

Jay

I was just constantly protecting myself. I was queer and hiding behind this illusion, and then you turned up. When you got here, you were the embodiment of 'the alien has landed!' Oh, there's another one! I want you to beam me up, to take me with you. That's what it felt like. I was the lost alien baby, then you came along with all your charisma, your vibrance and excitement and mental-ness, and your tenacity.

Glyn

You were the brightest, most creative light I had ever seen.

Jay

I didn't have a choice but to be creative. I grew up as a queer child in a world full of trauma. We were broke. Mum was a stripper, we lived with different people, I grew up with nothing so we had to create fun out of nothing. We had to build joy out of misery and sorrow. So we used to make things fun: imagination, counting coins, drawing on the sidewalk. Anything! Just fantasy. I was the eternal misfit.

Glyn

I remember that feeling of being misfits totally bonding us. I remember meeting your mum too. Do you mind talking about her?

Jay

She passed on so much of her creativity to me. In terms of her energy and life force, she was always 'do or die'. Her choice was to be an absolute missile of joy, or to embody sorrow and pain, or to just fade. No matter how much she was smashed, bashed and broken, she created an environment for us to feel loved and surrounded by creativity.

We talked about her dying before she died. So when she took her own life, there was no question in my mind that we loved each other. I didn't have stability and I guess that created its own issues, and I had abandonment issues or whatever because of it, but I learned my creativity from her. I learned to draw from her, to sew; I learned to be patient to be creative, that it was just about the *doing* and finding pleasure in the process and pursuit of creativity.

Glyn **Look at you now – a creative genius!**

Jay That's why I work as a creative, because the process is the enjoyable bit. If you're just interested in the end product, you will forever be disappointed. Perfection is unattainable and uninspiring. Where's the grit? I want imperfections! Where's the bollock hanging out the side of your pants so we can all laugh and feel human again? If it's so perfect, it's – I'm not going to say an illusion, because I think that can be a really beautiful thing, but I think delusion can be even better. Being lost in the delusion of feeling like you look like *that* bitch, having the most amazing time and pumping that energy out!

Glyn **A fabulous mantra: rip up the illusion and create the delusion!**

'PERFECTION
IS UNATTAINABLE
AND UNINSPIRING.
WHERE'S
THE GRIT?
I WANT
IMPERFECTIONS!'

THE JOY OF SMASHING THE CIS-TEM

It's taken years, but now I can say with my hand on my heart than nothing gives me more joy than smashing the cis-tem, bending gender and unleashing pure chaos with my merry gang of wonderful misfits. As weirdos, we get to opt out of bland, beige norms and create our own blueprints – so whatever you're into, whether it be bird-watching, knitting or skydiving, figure out how to channel every part of your personality into a vibrant life that is wholly, unequivocally yours.

For me, that means wriggling into ridiculous costumes and swinging from the rafters of clubs across the country with Sink The Pink, but equally it can mean running with my darling dog across a muddy field.

How could I write about joy without distilling some of the most exciting moments of Sink The Pink into the end of this chapter? Every single one of the moments in the following box means the world to me because they're representative of a life lived outside the shitty boxes that kept me down as a misfit. It took decades to get to this point, but when you have learned to embrace those bizarre, beautiful qualities once and for all, chasing your joy starts to feel a whole lot easier.

BORN AN ALIEN

THERE WAS THAT TIME...

... the music cut out in the club due to a power cut, and I led the entire club in singing Sisqo's 'Thong Song' while we all stripped.

... we decided to have a talcum powder rave, and shortly afterwards it all turned into thick, chalky slime that covered the entire club.

... when every major designer and stylist from the fashion world seemed to be in our humble little utopia... the following week, we were being shot by fashion legend Nick Knight for the front cover of Another Man magazine.

... the glorious drag creature Oozing Gloop decided to perform a Little Mermaid track with a giant, dead fish strapped to his penis... only to forget about the fish. The smell was foul!

... we wrapped our resident dancer Lucy Fizz up in gift wrap, and then made her stage dive – revealing a totally naked body and lots of misplaced rosettes!

... Bryan Adams turned up to the club... we've been turning him away ever since.

CHAPTER 5

FIND

YOUR

TRIBE

THE TRUE MAGIC OF

COMMUNITY

Whether it's the thrill of finding like-minded misfits online or the jolt of recognition that comes with actually seeing yourself represented positively, there's a feeling of true magic that comes with finding your tribe.

As misfits, we're alienated to the extent that we often believe there's nobody else like us in the world. If there *are* others like us, we're shown time and time again that they're miserable and destined to stay that way: not exactly what we want to see and hear! Mainstream media has a lot to answer for when it comes to poor representation and while the diversity of experiences shown on-screen is still so woefully in need of improvement, it's worth undertaking our own personal journeys to find the stories we need to survive.

Finding like-minded oddballs can give us the kick of validation we need to keep fighting through a world that tries to push us down, but that's not all it means to find your tribe. It could mean finding communities that share your interests too. Maybe you're desperate to find a group that shares your nerdiest obsessions, or you're in search of a local community that shares the same niche interests as you. From local IRL community groups to websites like Meetup and, of course, the endless list of local Facebook groups, there are ways to find your tribe – whether online or offline – and start to fill your life with other joyous, rebellious misfits.

FIND WHERE YOU'RE MEANT TO BE

I spent a lifetime trying to find where I fit in.

As a kid, the only time I really saw queer people was in rarefied glimpses of nightlife – the fabled disco-ball-lit dance floor of Studio 54, the chaos of the New York club kid scene and the snarling Fuck You! attitude of punk clubs around the world glimmered like sparkling lifelines, always vaguely in focus as I grew up and figured out the parts of myself I spent years trying to hide.

For so long, clubs felt both magnetically exciting and totally terrifying, but that fear didn't stop me going out and trying to find 'my people' as soon as I could.

I remember the first time I went out. I was seventeen years old (so obviously illegal!) but I was so desperate to discover *some* kind of club scene that I went to a Goth club in Bristol with my cousin. I still remember the smell of patchouli and cheap cider, but mainly I remember the fear that bristled through my every pore as I took my first steps into the great unknown. Surely this would be my scene – a room of misfits embracing self-expression was, on paper, exactly what I had been looking for. Yet back then, I was so uncomfortable in my own skin that I spent the whole night taking shots of a mysterious blue drink – probably not the best idea, in hindsight. Needless to say, I didn't even reach midnight. Instead, I vomited blue puke all over a stranger's lap!

From that point onwards, the search was on. It was a wild, eventful series of trial-and-error moments to find where I truly thrived. I tried to be a raver for a while, but I realised I didn't actually like rave music – a pretty key component! I went to countless gigs and watched bands that I adored play live, but nobody came to speak to me. I stood there nodding myself into obscurity, shuffling awkwardly to the sounds of my favourite songs.

All the while, I was wrestling with the difficulties of that signature queer experience: the coming-out moment. My coming-out story is unsurprisingly extra – I moved all the way to Australia to do it! I had decided that only with a change of scenery could I become the magnificent, confident peacock I yearned to become. In my eyes, that trip was the first step on my path towards self-discovery; it represented me flinging back the curtain and stepping into my truth.

I had it all planned out in my mind: I would go to the local gay club, and as I stepped through those hallowed doors, everyone would turn to look at me and thank me for finally finding them. I believed that everyone would get to know my name, that I would never be the same again. Right? Wrong! In reality, I stood in a dimly lit corner of the club all night, my knees trembling. I was too scared to even make eye contact with any strangers, let alone talk to them.

One drink, two drinks, three drinks, shot, four drinks, five drinks, SHIT! Next thing I know, I'm face down in a stranger's house (the 'friendly' barman) feeling anything but self-acceptance. This was *not* the plan – I needed something more, something different.

It was a wild, eventful series of trial-and-error moments to find where I truly thrived.

CLUB GUILTY PLEASURES

It's all well and good knowing what you *don't* want, but what about what you *do* want? Thinking about what drives you, what makes you happy and what makes you tick will help you figure out the qualities and interests that can lead you to other misfits, and a good way to do that is to conjure up the magnificent dream of your very own club.

I want you to create a space that is full of all your guilty pleasures, where you can have your dream night out. Imagine you are creating a space that represents you at your wildest, baddest, riskiest, silliest and most ridiculous self.

Chuck taste, judgement and fear out the window, *then* you can start putting your club together.

Imagine a night with no limits and let your mind run wild.

- What is the club called?
- What does this club represent?
- Who is on the guest list? They can be people you know or famous people, dead or alive.
- Imagine the soundtrack. Remember it's YOUR club so play whatever you want. Curate a playlist that sums you up.
- Who's performing?
- Will there be a theme?
- What are you going to wear?
- Will there be some kind of eye-catching, über-memorable moment, à la Bianca Jagger arriving at Studio 54 on a white horse?

BE PATIENT WITH YOURSELF

My earliest attempts at stepping into my fabulous, misfit self ultimately left me feeling more hollow and ashamed than all the years I spent in the closet. That fateful, shitty first night in a gay club actually added to my already-existing trauma, and this is something that *all* misfits should know: your journey towards self-acceptance will never be straightforward and linear.

I left that club feeling no more prepared to tell those I loved who I truly was, so I carried on being too scared to go back to nightclubs and too paralysed with fear to say those three fateful words: I am gay.

At that point, I could have given up and tiptoed back into the closet to stay for the rest of my life.

Yet soon afterwards, I found myself in a truly transformative situation – although I didn't know it at the time. After several months in Australia, I was running out of money and still barely had any friends, but none of this seemed as bad to me as moving back to Bristol. I decided I needed to get a job and meet new people, so I trawled around local shops with a shit, almost-empty CV. After a few miserable days I slumped, defeated, on a bench and suddenly heard cackles of laughter coming from a brightly coloured café – in retrospect, it was one of those 'a-ha' moments that are easy to miss if you're not looking for them.

I puffed out my chest like an over-confident, slightly dishevelled pigeon and wandered inside to be greeted by an older gentleman dressed in light, pastel-coloured linen, his wild, curly hair whipping in the breeze created by the rather fabulous fan he kept wafting through the air. Serendipitously, he was the owner of the café. He offered me a job on the spot, and Aunty Donald – as I came to know him – became one of the most important mentors in my life, shaping me into the gay man I am today. It turns out the café was a regular watering hole for fabulous queers including Bex, a hippy lesbian, Marina, a bona fide nightclub queen and Cam, a Shania Twain impersonator who acted as a mother to us all.

This motley crew of glorious weirdos became my chosen family; they encouraged and corrupted me in equal measures! From here on out, I didn't just become gay, I became *really* fucking gay!

An Ongoing Journey

My trip unfortunately had to come to an end a few months later, but the experience lit a flame in my belly and gave me a tantalising taste of how brilliant it felt to be totally, unapologetically myself. Yet I was living a double life – in Australia I was a crop-top-wearing, go-go-dancing, flaming homosexual, while everyone at home was under the impression I had a girlfriend and was working in a *nice* restaurant! On the plane ride home, I was filled with dread, and fear that my family would cut me out of their lives when they learned the truth.

Essentially, I had to come out *again* – and this is something queer people in particular aren't told enough. If you're within the LGBTQ+ community, you don't just come out once and have done with it. On every application form, in every new, intimate interaction, we have to 'come out' all over again, and experience the same lingering dread that comes with it.

The next few days were a blur. I told family and then friends, all the while feeling numb and exhausted. At first, I was angry at people around me for making me talk about my experiences, but then I realised: it had taken me so long to understand and then accept this part of myself, so I needed to give them the same time and space to come to terms with it too.

In retrospect, I was super impatient – maybe even a bit of a brat! – but my family not only came around to it, they celebrated me, loved me, pushed me and joked with me.

'TAKE A STEP TO UNDERSTAND YOURSELF'

It didn't happen overnight, and not everyone's story will be wrapped up with such a neat, loving bow. There are plenty of resources (listed later in the book; see pages 168–70) for those of you who aren't fortunate enough to have these support networks, and the wonderful teams behind these services can become part of your tribe too, if you let them. Opening up and reaching out can be an essential first step towards surrounding yourself with people who care about you and want the best for you. Remember the path leading up to this might be messy, winding and sometimes exhausting. Patience is key, but each day will bring you a step closer to understanding yourself and then sharing those lessons with those you love.

WHAT'S IN A SAFER...

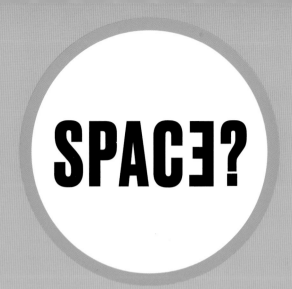

SPACE?

We've already established that the world can be extremely hostile to us misfits for no good reason, so where do we go? How do we find our own tribes without having to navigate yet more difficulties? The answer lies in safer spaces.

Their Origins

Especially within nightlife, these physical pockets of utopia have been around for centuries, we've just never called them 'safer spaces'. From the ballrooms of Harlem, where legendary queer chosen families gathered to dance, drink and strut their self-made runways, to the so-called 'molly houses' of eighteenth- and nineteenth-century Britain, which offered shelter to gay men seeking sex and companionship, 'safer spaces' have been around for centuries.

Sometimes, they're born of necessity – like the 'sip-ins'[1] pioneered by gay men who were routinely barred from nightclubs in the mid-1960s, or Casa Susanna[2], a secret weekend retreat where members of the trans community could express themselves without fear, which operated predominantly in the early 1960s. More recent examples include nights like Pxssy Palace, specifically designed for queer people of colour who still experience racism in queer settings, and the various 'safe spaces' on university campuses, which allow marginalised people to come together without fear of having their identities debated, dissected or insulted by other students.

Learning by Example

In the last few years in particular, we've started to realise that no space is guaranteed to be 'safe' – hence the switch within activist circles to the term 'safer spaces'. There are ways to work towards this safety, however. Staff training at venues is one way, for example teaching security guards not to harass a trans person if they haven't updated their gender marker on their legal ID. Another is to write a manifesto or a mission statement that explains in clear, unambiguous terms that discrimination won't be accepted, and then working with club-goers to stamp out any situations that arise on the night.

When it came to launching Sink The Pink, we learned from these examples to make our world as inclusive and welcoming as possible. Not all of this was about policies and check-ups – one of my favourite parts of any Sink The Pink night is a magical booth called Glitter My Shitter, which later became known as Salon de Slag. Because dressing up in your fanciest glad-rags and actually getting to the club in full drag often means risking assault or judgement from strangers, we created this budget fashion sanctuary on site, which is packed full of glitter, sparkles, grease-paint and every ridiculous costume you could imagine – it means that our friends can get glammed up without worrying about what the world thinks of them, and they can live their best lives with like-minded, wonderful weirdos.

Space to Let Loose

Safer spaces aren't about gatekeeping – they're about providing outlets to misfits who desperately need them. In the UK alone, there were more than 105,000 hate crimes[3] committed in the year ending March 2020, marking yet another increase in rates which have been steadily rising over the last decade. Homicide rates of trans people – especially trans women of colour – also continue to rise year in, year out, in countries like the US[4] and Brazil in particular, so it should come as no surprise that communities constantly made to feel vulnerable and fearful for just being themselves are reliant on safer spaces to really let loose.

Safer spaces aren't about gatekeeping – they're about providing outlets to misfits who desperately need them.

This doesn't just have to mean going to a nightclub, either. You can always seek out local community centres, pay-what-you-can cafés and grassroots organisations that aim to provide shelter and refuge for misfits otherwise left in the cold. From soup kitchens to subsidised art classes, there are various alternatives – usually built on socialist values of mutual aid and community care – that specifically aim to provide safer spaces outside of nightlife settings. Especially given that marginalised communities[5] are disproportionately vulnerable to substance abuse, organisers are constantly brewing inventive, innovative ways to transfer the magic of safer spaces to sober settings.

Sometimes, even the safer spaces that do exist aren't safe for everyone. Lady Phyll, co-founder of UK Black Pride, channelled her determination to create a genuinely inclusive safe space for LGBTQ+ people of colour into one of the country's biggest, most brilliant annual events. Alongside a dedicated team, Phyll works tirelessly to produce a yearly extravaganza, as well as activities throughout the year, both inside the country and out.

These activities are all intended to promote and advocate for the spiritual, emotional and intellectual health and wellbeing of the communities that UK Black Pride represents. Overleaf, she writes a letter to her community, exploring the importance of connection.

LADY PHYLL'S LETTER TO HER COMMUNITY

My darling misfits,

I know what you're thinking (because I'm thinking it, too): 'Black girls don't get to be "misfits".' And you're right. Of all the things the world marks upon us, it is never the label 'misfit'. But there is perhaps no greater or marvellous misfit than the Black woman.

The dictionary defines a 'misfit' as 'a person whose behaviour or attitude sets them apart from others in an uncomfortably conspicuous way.' Of all that we could unpack here, not least who gets to define what, I want to linger on 'uncomfortably conspicuous'. I remember examining my body, with those laser-vision eyes we develop as teenagers. Conscious of my growing breasts and widening hips; conscious that my Black skin made me so clearly visible in the world, I thought of all the ways I could be different.

I thought of all the girls who moved through the world as if invisible, and longed to be able to hide. But hiding, for me, required a dulling of myself and my shine that I found unbearable. It meant denying my grandmother's legacy, the forthright determination she gave me by example, and the tender, tough love she showered me with. It meant being something other than myself.

Of course, I would emerge into a world not designed for my thriving and I would encounter others who didn't see the glory I began to see in myself. And so sometimes I have been silent to prevent others' discomfort. Sometimes, I have made myself smaller to avoid the tension that pulses through a room when I dare challenge someone. But what I've learned, over and over again, is that silent or dull, quiet or small, my very presence in a room, on a street or in a magazine will elicit discomfort from those who don't believe Black women have entitlement to the same world as they do. And so I speak, and I walk proud, and I believe in the very fibre of my queer, Black being that I deserve to be here.

So do you. We are misfits.

And good for us! Who wants to belong to the world as it is? Who wants to blend in when blending in means being wilfully blind to the horrors of our time? Who wants to make themselves small when we have giants to defeat?

If being a misfit means I embody my worth, and I refuse to be talked down, and I stand up for what's right, especially when it's hard, then a misfit I will be. If being a misfit means being fully present to the violence so that we can work towards the safety and beauty we all deserve, then so be it.

I will run through these streets, as I have done, shouting the good gospel for all those who can't yet raise their voices: 'The misfits shall inherit the Earth!'

THE MISFITS SHALL INHERIT THE EARTH!

BUILD YOUR OWN SPACES

Like the thousands lucky enough to have experienced UK Black Pride, sometimes we misfits stumble upon an event, a venue, a community or even a forum that simply feels like home.

After moving home from Australia, I continued to experiment with different 'scenes' and years of self-discovery followed before I eventually landed in East London. One fateful night, I received a text message from my friend Jacob saying, 'Come to Gay Bingo.' I had pretty much tried everything already, and I at least knew how to play Bingo – I had played it regularly with my family as a kid – so I thought, 'Fuck it, why not?' That night led me down a path I've continued on ever since.

As we stepped into a grimy warehouse, I realised this wouldn't be like the gloriously camp, old-school bingo halls of my youth! I saw sweaty, glamorous creatives dancing in every corner of the room; the most beautiful mix of humans I've ever seen under one roof. Decked out in full gender-fuck regalia, there were three queens on the stage: Jonny Woo, John Sizzle and Ma Butcher.

These East London icons were anything but conventional. They ran this institution, and made everyone who set foot in the grotty, industrial venue feel like it was their home. Do what you want, act how you want: they led by example. I remember Jonny performing the old-school Broadway classic 'I'm Gonna Wash That Man Right Outa My Hair' from *South Pacific* while lying in a kids' paddling pool. John Sizzle walked out, pulled out his sizzler and pissed all over Woo's wig!

My jaw hit the floor; this was wild! It was fearless. It felt like *me*. Over time, they took me under their dirty, beautifully matted wings, corrupted me and gave me the courage to fuck things up on my own terms. From that point onwards, my life would never be the same again.

When it came to launching Sink The Pink, these wacky, hedonistic experiences made up the backbone of what we wanted: something wild, inclusive and raucous, in the best way possible. For years, Sink The Pink was under constant attack for being too trashy, too camp or too stupid – so now you know which troublemakers are to blame! Naturally, I followed in the footsteps of these brilliant weirdos – in fact, I grabbed all those opinions and wore them like a badge of honour.

Too trashy? You've not seen anything yet – that accusation spurred me along to go even bigger, and before anyone knew it, I was fully naked in the club playing a game of Kerplunk with straws up my bum!

Don't believe me? To sum up the true euphoria of Sink The Pink, see the next page for a few quotes from like-minded misfits who came to shake their butts, glitter their shitters and dance the night away with our colourful band of weirdos.

I'll always remember coming to Sink The Pink for the first time and feeling instantly at home. Glyn was doing a catwalk show, and the drag queen Jacqui Potato walked straight to the front of the stage with a real look of pride on her face. The next thing I knew, she had pulled a frying pan out of her bag, squatted above it and laid an egg – an actual soft-boiled egg!
Tam*, *Manchester

I've lost my keys, my mind, my clothes and more at Sink The Pink! I came alive when I discovered that place; the freedom and pure, effervescent joy it gives me is comparable only to an orgasm!
Charli T, London

The first time I attended a Sink The Pink show was at the Bethnal Green Working Men's Club. It completely changed my view of masculinity. It opened my eyes to gender-fuck and how to deconstruct gender; that became the start of a really fun adventure for me. Since then, I've never looked back!
Ramrayn, London

As a queer kid who adored the Spice Girls, growing up I had a tough time finding people that represented me. I loved the strength they gave me, so as an adult I decided to go see Melanie C at Times Square for World Pride. The Sink The Pink collective performed with her, and it was a moment I'll never forget – an actual Spice Girl with five people that looked like and truly represented me. It was a life-affirming moment!
Leo, New York

REPRESENTATIoN
REQUIRƎD

Finding communities in real life is one thing, but various media industries play a huge role in our understandings of 'normality' too.

It's hard to understand yourself if you never see your role models represented. There's an age-old saying that 'you can't be what you can't see', and for many misfits across the world, it's a sentiment that rings true – we're told there are too many barriers to our happiness, that we're too weird or anomalous to succeed. Essentially, that we're not 'normal', let alone excellent.

When you don't see bodies, stories or communities that look like yours on-screen, there comes this nagging sense that the world doesn't want you there; that you're not worthy of representation. Advertisements sell us false ideals of 'perfection' which still centre on thin, able-bodied, conventionally attractive white characters, whereas television, film and fashion haven't yet nailed a sweet spot when it comes to showing a diversity of bodies, ages, genders, abilities and races.

How Diverse is Hollywood?

According to the 2021 Hollywood Diversity Report[6], 2020 was a 'watershed moment' for diversity – although there's still little in the way of long-term planning to ensure this becomes the norm rather than the exception. Each year the debates around whether cis actors should play trans roles are also reignited, yet trans actors across the board are still often boxed into narrow archetypes and rarely given the freedom to play cis roles; elsewhere, landmark castings of non-white actors are still met with racist abuse.

When it was announced in November 2020 that Lashana Lynch had been cast in a leading role as a 007 agent in the James Bond film *No Time to Die,* she reportedly disabled her social media accounts for a week due to racist backlash. 'If it were another Black woman cast in the role, it would have been the same conversation, she would have got the same attacks, the same abuse,' she later said[7].

It's also worth noting that these aforementioned supposed wins for representation on-screen often don't reflect what's going on behind the cameras. In a landmark study entitled 'Hollywood Diversity Report 2020: A Tale of Two Hollywoods'[8], stats showed that in 2019, only 14.4 per cent of films with a theatrical release were directed by people of colour. Elsewhere, much was made about the fact that 15.5 per cent of films were directed by women, a statistic cited by publications and celebrated as a 'record high'. Yet even within these statistics, study authors Dr Darnell Hunt and Dr Ana-Christina Ramón found that women of colour were hugely under-represented compared to their white counterparts, and that women across the board 'remained under-represented by a factor of more than three to one in this employment arena in 2019'.

These studies show there's still a disconnect between what we see on screen and what goes on behind the scenes. In other words, we misfits aren't always given the chance to tell our own stories, and we certainly aren't always paid or respected equally when we do.

Mainstream Media

It's not just about Hollywood, either. Especially in the UK, mainstream media is a transphobic shit-show and peddles dangerous myths and rehashes disgusting debates about the 'validity' of trans people like they're some kind of abstract, philosophical concept. Trans communities have always been here – you just wouldn't know it because queer archives like the Institute of Sexual Science, which documented a rich trans history in pre-war Berlin, have been literally burned to the ground. Black actors and comedians have spoken openly about racism in the UK film and television industries too – in 2020, David Harewood revealed his agent encouraged Black actors to move to the US as there 'isn't an industry to support [them]'[9]; in 2021, comedian Gina Yashere discussed being used as a token on UK TV shows, and described an 'insidious pathetic limp handshake of British establishment racism'.[10] In other words, the discrimination is so heavily coded that it's often brushed under the rug.

Luckily, there are advocates creating their own representation, busting harmful myths and telling their stories with a tongue-in-cheek attitude. I'm lucky enough to call Dani St James, co-founder of UK trans+ charity Not a Phase, a friend. Like me, she's weathered enough bullshit for her 'misfit' status to last a lifetime – but now she's taking that experience and using it to build bridges with other trans folk who haven't yet found their tribe.

PHONE A FRIEND

DANI ST JAMES

Glyn   I feel like we're quite similar, in that we've both created larger-than-life characters for ourselves over the years.

Dani   I think that's a conditioned response of self-protection, because we've been constantly demonised for who we *actually* are. If you're constantly told that who you are is wrong, creating a character can feel like a shield. It also ties into my trans identity. Everything I have and am was not given to me, it was cultivated. I could have turned into any type of woman, so I was working out who I was going to become – that takes time! It takes years to let go of these constraints that you've built up around yourself.

Glyn   Tell me more about what being trans means to you.

Dani

I think there's something that separates my journey from the trans mainstream because I resent the idea of 'being born in the wrong body'. I never felt that way; I just feel like I was given a few extra hurdles, but it's such a blessing that I managed to jump them, because the alternative was being a fucking miserable gay boy. When I was a teenager, I just thought I was a gay man because I saw no trans representation. Every gay man I could see, I emulated.

My dad used to say when I was little that I was just like David Bowie or Boy George, and so did my mum – she was this punk in the 1980s. They thought I was this gender-bender extraordinaire, and they thought that was quite fab!

Glyn

How did your identity develop as you grew up?

Dani

I was lucky – I went to a Catholic school that had gender-neutral toilets and a unisex uniform. Teachers even let me do PE classes with the girls, because they realised I worked better in that environment. Even when I told my mum I wanted to wear make-up and paint my nails, she took me into town, bought me a load of make-up and said, 'Well, you can't have the shit stuff!' So I never felt like I was trapped in the wrong body, because there was no entrapment. It was just 'OK, this is who you are – we'll work the rest out later.'

Glyn You're a big advocate for visibility with Not a Phase now – how did that come about?

Dani When I first met a trans woman, it was like a mirror being held up to me. I feel like I've been afforded so much privilege on so many levels, but in terms of the trans world, I have passing privilege – I can walk into a room of board executives and they accept me because of the way I look and the tone of my voice. I have so much more access than so many trans people, so Not a Phase stemmed from me asking how I could take that and pay it forward.

Glyn Finally, do you think it's a good time to take pride in being a misfit?

Dani There's never been a more important time, because I think if I had seen someone like me when I was nine years old, I would have known then. We see more kids coming out as trans or gay because they're seeing themselves reflected more in media, their peer group, adverts and even politics. We're having our day, but with that comes a duty to put ourselves out there. We need to lay our cards down so the next generation can see and know who we are.

THE POLITICAL IMPORTANCE OF TRIBES

There are so many benefits to finding your own kindred spirits: from sharing your own experiences to delving deep into mutual passions and seeing life reflected through another lens you can relate to, there's a lot to be said for finding your tribe. Yet there's also political utility in seeking out like-minded misfits, especially if your shared experiences mean you're fighting largely towards the same political goals.

During the 1970s, when mainstream feminism was beginning to splinter and its lack of inclusivity was becoming more evident than ever before, a group of Black feminist scholars and activists formed the Combahee River Collective to specifically ensure the political needs of Black women were being considered and fought for within feminism. In a 1977 manifesto[11], they laid the foundations of what we now know as 'identity politics', writing: 'This focus on our own oppression is embodied in the concept of identity politics. We believe that the most profound and potentially the most radical politics come directly out of our own identity, as opposed to working to end somebody else's oppression.'

We should all come together and collectively push for change.

Solidarity and allyship are still hugely important, but these women recognised that those who didn't understand their struggles were less likely to fight for their cause, so they banded together and tirelessly advocated for the rights of other Black women like them. Misfits have a deep-rooted understanding of what it means to walk through a world that tries to shrink us, as well as what the obstacles placed in our way are. Instead of explaining that to people who either don't understand or don't want to, this logic suggests we should all come together and collectively push for change. There are clear political benefits to this: it builds strength in numbers and fosters power between people who actively know what it's like to be marginalised and to struggle. Finding your own tribe of raucous, radical misfits could be the key you need to unlock long-lasting socio-political change.

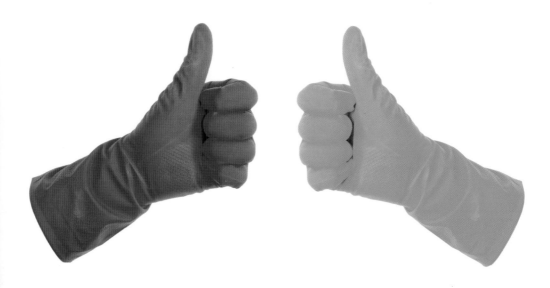

CHAPTER 6

START A
REVOL

UTION

FIGHT FOR MORE

The ultimate, hidden truth of the world is that it is something that we make, and could just as easily make differently.[1]

These are the words of David Graeber, a radical thinker who saw through society's bullshit and, with this one quote, gave misfits worldwide a mantra to live by. Without veering into sticky, academic language about 'constructs' and 'systems', let's just put it this way: we live in societies full of rules, regulations and norms which are all created and upheld by institutions. These create complex systems of thinking – race, gender, justice, for example – which might seem fixed and unchangeable. Yet this isn't true; we're just subconsciously told not to think too much about this stuff in case we start to realise that the norms we're told to think of as absolute 'truths' can come unravelled if we start asking different questions. This isn't just about law and politics, it's everything – from the way we think about not just ourselves but about the world at large.

This gospel truth has taught punks, rebels and misfits around the globe to believe that so much more is possible, to believe in the fight for more.

Let's be real, here: most of us, most of the time, are really fucking overwhelmed. Life can be a *lot*. That means that we misguidedly, defeatistly, accept what we see and find; we don't question and we don't analyse. Yet the world is something that was made and can be made differently. You might not have had much of a say up until now, but why shouldn't you think about how you can play a part in that brand new shaping process from here on out?

The ultimate, hidden truth of the world is that it is something that we make, and could just as easily make differently.

WHAT'S IN A REVOLUTION

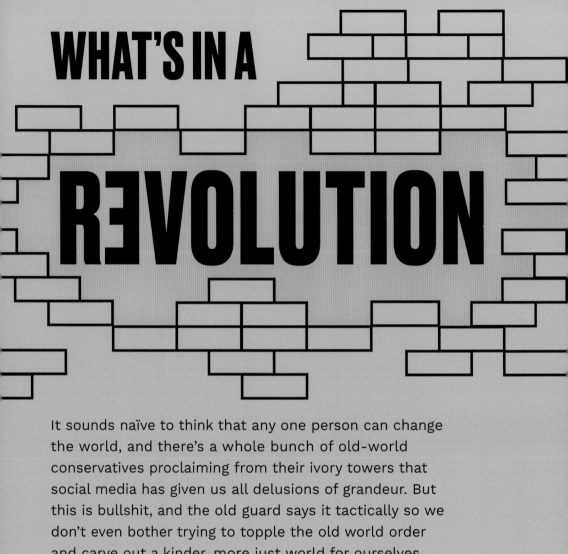

It sounds naïve to think that any one person can change the world, and there's a whole bunch of old-world conservatives proclaiming from their ivory towers that social media has given us all delusions of grandeur. But this is bullshit, and the old guard says it tactically so we don't even bother trying to topple the old world order and carve out a kinder, more just world for ourselves. The fact is that activism works, action is powerful and there is no one way to start a revolution. Activism doesn't have to mean storming a government building – in fact, it's probably best if you don't – or single-handedly changing the law. This tendency to think on a dizzying, global scale is what can make the whole notion of starting a revolution feel too daunting to even try.

So, let's reframe the question: what is a revolution, and what can you do to help it along?

In a nutshell, it's change. Everything is about change. The person you are today is different from who you were yesterday. We're all in a constant state of flux, evolving into new amalgamations of ourselves at breakneck speed, like gorgeous, dynamic Pokémon. Yet even as we rocket through this never-ending cycle of development, there'll be a handful of qualities that anchor us, that make us who we are.

For us misfits, these are usually the parts of ourselves we've been told to shrink or taught to hate. They're the attributes that earn us that label of difference, and hopefully by now, you're at the point of fully embracing them and asking how you can help fellow misfits feel the same way. An example is the constant stream of housing and medical fundraisers that are shared within networks of queer and trans people of colour, which are designed to give financial and emotional support to those who are vulnerable or struggling. Then, there's the gift of representation – writing our own stories as misfits can empower those who don't usually see themselves and their lives depicted with any kind of nuance, excitement or joy, so even launching a zine or flexing your artistic muscles can give much-needed validation. Sober safer spaces are also a great idea – whether it's a local centre in the community or creating moderated online chat-rooms for fellow misfits to vent and share resources, there are plenty of ways to make incremental change that can genuinely touch the lives of other misfits.

Of course, on a political level, some misfits have more to lose than others; some of us have fundamental human rights at stake. Before you dive headfirst into starting your own revolution, it's important to know yourself wholly: what are your values, principles and belief systems?

A KINDER, MORE JUST WORLD

FIND
YOUR

FIGHT

Let's tap back into the power of dreaming big and imagine, just for a second, that you're a world leader with the potential to change anything fizzing at your fingertips. What would you do? Maybe you'd enforce universal free healthcare and enshrine protections for fellow misfits into laws across the globe; on the other hand, perhaps you'd lodge your tongue firmly in your cheek and gift every household a free pet lizard!

No matter what your goals are, mentally step into your zaniest, most colourful zoot suit and let your imagination run wild. As the untamed, unrestrained misfit president of the world, what would your policies look like?

Here are a few examples to get your creative juices flowing:
- State-sanctioned reward schemes for excessive use of (eco-friendly, of course!) glitter
- Safe, accessible housing for everyone who needs it, regardless of income
- Judgement-free education which teaches us all about neurodiversity
- Abolition of gendered uniform codes
- Mandatory screenings of John Waters' queer films in schools worldwide
- An annual Nerd Appreciation Day, where we all lean unashamedly into our most wonderfully niche interests
- Replace the national anthem with a Destiny's Child medley.

You get the gist... now, give it a go!

LOOK TO YOUR IDOLS

As a teenager growing up in a house filled with siblings, having the place to myself was such a rarity. Yet one night, long before the internet (strange to think, I know!), I found myself home alone scrolling through TV channels when a gloriously quirky, outrageously colourful artist popped onto my screen.

This magnificent creature was unlike anything I had ever seen before; meticulously placed swirls of paint trailed from his bald head down to his forehead, his face covered in a riotous mix of bruise-red blush, sapphire paint and heavy, carefully stencilled blocks of black. Little did I know back then, I had stumbled upon a documentary about the life and work of club kid legend Leigh Bowery.

For those who don't know, Leigh was synonymous with London in the 1980s – he was the gender-bending queen of the scene, darling! The larger-than-life performance artist, born in Australia, captivated clubbers across the city with his jaw-dropping costumes and totally bonkers performances – he once 'gave birth' to his wife Nicola Bateman (Leigh always described himself as gay but was incredibly close to Nicola) while wearing a white gimp mask, fashioning a makeshift umbilical cord out of chain-linked sausages! Needless to say, I was mesmerised.

Leigh went on to launch his infamous club night, Taboo, and cement his reputation as a cultural icon. Although his life was sadly taken too soon by AIDS in 1994, his legacy is still felt around the world – and in my eyes at least, he's the ultimate misfit.

Watching his documentary felt so incredibly dangerous. I was staring into a future I desperately longed for while I, sat on my sofa in innercity

Bristol, was still deep in hiding. His Fuck You attitude gave me the fire I needed to push back against shame and step straight into my weirdness, and finding your idols will do the same for you. Whether it's an activist campaigning for policy change or a pop superstar who encourages you to come out of your shell and rebel against social norms, misfit idols have laid the foundations for today's provocateurs – and yes, that can be you! – to go against the grain and nudge the needle of what society thinks is 'acceptable'.

The list really is endless – from the likes of Malala Yousafzai, a Pakistani education activist who became the youngest person to ever earn a Nobel Peace Prize, to world-renowned climate crisis campaigner Greta Thunberg, there are plenty of change-makers to look up to and learn from. For me, it was Leigh Bowery's determination to create space for fellow weirdos to thrive that inspired my own mini-revolution, and it's one that's ongoing today.

GO AGAINST THE GRAIN

PUNK PLEDGE BY YUNGBLUD

I pledge allegiance to the weirdos, the freaks, to all of the strange and abnormal creatures who twist ideas of normality into brilliant new shapes. To anyone brave enough to reject the bullshit forced on us by society, I give you my undying respect. To everyone who stands together in the face of the ordinary and tells it to fuck right off, I give you my life!

We aren't encouraged to be weird and wonderful, or to seize hold of what makes us unique and shout it from the rooftops. Yet to be unique is to be free, and to be free is, to me, what it means to be successful. It's what it means to be an artist too; everything I create bleeds with my own personality, my own DNA. If I had listened to everyone who had ever tried to bring me down, I wouldn't be the person I am today.

The goal is to keep becoming exactly who I was always meant to be, and to hurtle headfirst into that journey on my own terms. Everyone deserves to know how exhilarating the feeling is to step into your strange, so go ahead. Celebrate sex. Celebrate people. Celebrate yourself! Your weirdness is your biggest strength, and shoving that in society's face is the best way to move through life. And always remember, never let anybody undermine your individuality. The chances are that they damn well envy it.

To anyone
brave enough
to reject the
bullshit forced
on us by society,
I give you my
undying respect.

STARTING OUR

R3VOLUTIₒN

I think the biggest revolutions happen when we are making big changes in our own lives, which might have unintentional or unexpected effects. That's how it happened with me. I had reached such a miserable, disillusioned place that I genuinely felt I had hit rock bottom. In my eyes, I had spent a huge chunk of my life wearing a mask and not being true to myself.

I had two options: either admit defeat, or run headfirst into the dangerous unknown. Naturally, I chose the latter. I took that step by planning wild, wacky new experiences with my partner-in-crime Amy, and from that one decision, I ended up meeting my fellow Sink The Pink recruits. We all shared deep feelings of frustration at how terribly the world treats misfits, but we didn't just want *acceptance* – we knew that we all deserved to be wholly, truly celebrated.

The Sink The Pink Bandits

We started a revolution by saying no to society's bullshit, by challenging the status quo of the stale club scene and by putting ourselves front and centre. We stood for so much by just being authentically ourselves, and by never apologising for who we are. We demanded respect! Through this, we became poster children for trans rights, gender-bending, drag and more. We never intentionally set out to do any of this; we were just brave enough to listen to the fire burning deep inside, and loyal enough to lift each other up through the tough days.

All we had was an inkling that, if we could gather a group of weird, wonderful bandits with a shared vision, then we could create our own joy. Even in clubs, meant to be these havens of escapism from the daily grind of reality, we weren't seeing that zany, effervescent spirit we're still so determined to find. Instead, we saw sanitised spaces gate-kept by people applying labels and enforcing dress codes and restrictive policies. We wanted to stick two fingers up to that, but instead of spending years planning it, we just ran full force into it. Don't overthink, just do! Our revolution remains a playful, primal one, defined by a no-fucks-given attitude and the freedom to take up space.

Before we knew it, what started as a straightforward mission to have some fucking *fun* turned into something way bigger. It became our own revolution. Sink The Pink became a collective of energy, a cacophony of noise that kept building until it became disruptive, and then political – without us even realising or aiming to do that in the first place. When you lean into being totally, unapologetically yourself and then give other people the freedom to do the same, there's this fabulous snowball effect. When that train starts running, it's hard to get off.

The process of unlearning and questioning everything can have a similar snowball effect. Activism and values are too often framed as static and unchanging, but there's power in admitting when you're wrong and constantly re-analysing to see where you stand. Living life as an outsider, an eternal voyeur, I learned not to think in black-and-white terms. Misfits spend years in the margins of the page, never quite centred. We spend that time questioning, finding ways to move past the 'either/or' boxes we're given and push deeper, searching for the spectrums and the spaces in-between.

SPECTRUMS AND THE SPACES IN-BETWEEN

Our Sink The Pink family also just *really* hated feeling constrained, or like we didn't have the freedom to be or behave how we wanted. Some misfits find comfort in rules and routines, but for the Sink The Pink family, we shared an added layer of being talked down to, misunderstood and working shitty jobs. As frustrated misfits, we banded together to break out and create our own worlds with our own rules.

It's Your Turn

Your revolution might look like this too. It's easy to get carried away by momentum and determination once you've figured out what you truly stand for, but the most important thing is to check in with yourself constantly:

- What's your motivation?
- What's the impetus for doing this now?
- Who and what are you doing this for?
- What's your end goal?

If those reasons are selfish, the wheels will fall off and everything will turn to shit. Usually, those motivations aren't sustainable, either – you might reach one breakthrough, but you need a bigger driving force to ensure that progress is kept up, so really interrogate your reasons.

For us, transitioning those breakthrough moments into lasting action was the truly difficult part. Maybe we misfits are allowed to find occasional moments of euphoria, but the world wants them to be exactly that – momentary, and usually monetised. We managed to avoid that by chasing an energy instead, and bringing together our beautiful band of weirdos to form a coven where vulnerability was not only welcomed, it was encouraged. That's how the different Sink The Pink members all found each other – we're fragile, but also brave. Vulnerable, but strong enough to live life on our own terms without second thoughts.

When you start actively working towards your revolution, the blanks will be filled in as you go along. The only missions that we had in mind were to eliminate labels, spread joy and create a space of unfiltered, almost child-like freedom, one where freaks and outcasts could gather and be unapologetically wild. I now spend much of my life surrounded by beautiful oddballs, but I'll never forget the first time I saw a plethora of sweaty, painted bodies on the Sink The Pink dance floor, a sea of glorious weirdos dressed in rag-tag, DIY costumes embracing each other and dancing their cares away.

Make Technology Your Friend

Although our revolution was born of frustration and straight-up fucking *boredom*, this isn't always the case. Sometimes, these revolutions are way more explicitly political, and they're launched by activists literally fighting for their lives, and for some of these activists, boredom would be a luxury. Instead they have to use whatever means they can to carve out a space for themselves.

It might have its downsides, but technology has played a huge role in this over the last two decades. In early 2011, a month after protests erupted across Tunisia due to policing so corrupt that a fruit seller set himself alight after having his goods confiscated, demonstrations began cropping up in countries across the Middle East.[2] Even as national governments scrambled to shut down phone networks, activists used clever social media tactics to organise protests and share them with the world, resulting in what we now know as the 'Arab Spring'. More recently, activists used hashtags to spread key details in the wake of George Floyd's 2020 murder by police officer Derek Chauvin, mobilising a #BlackLivesMatter movement across the world.[3]

More of us than ever now have the tools at our disposal to start our own mini-revolutions – whether that means protesting injustice, sharing resources or linking with other communities to protect each other, revolution is attainable if you focus your aim and ask yourself what you can realistically change. Alone, we might feel helpless. But as a global army of misfits with the fire of frustration burning deep in our stomachs, we can collectively push for a fairer, more just world.

AN HOMAGE TO THE ACCIDƎNTAL ACTIVISTS

There's a big difference between wanting change and needing it. I'll give you an example: back in 2019, the organisers of São Paulo Pride reached out to ask if our beautiful group of misfits would come with Sporty Spice to join their world-famous celebration. We were all absolutely floored – of course we *would* come!

As the weeks ticked by, we all started to understand exactly why this particular Pride celebration was so important. Pride has always been radical – it's held in June each year to mark the anniversary of the Stonewall Riots, a series of clashes in New York City in 1969, which erupted when the crowd of largely queer, trans and gender non-conforming patrons of colour fought back against the police, who would routinely raid the bar and arrest them. They fought for their lives, launching everything from (depending on which accounts you read) bricks to high heels at the cops, sowing the seeds for what would soon blossom into a global queer liberation movement. Each year, we recognise this history, celebrating the progress we have made and continually campaigning for the change that still needs to come.

Since being elected in 2018, Brazilian President Jair Bolsonaro has been working to roll back the hard-earned rights of queer communities in his country, going so far as to call for a ban on Pride parades altogether. Our place was right in the middle of this chaos, on a gigantic moving stage being pulled down one of the city's biggest freeways.

We were hit by this incredible wall of energy, a kind of euphoria mixed with sheer fury. This was the energy of people who were desperately

We were hit by this incredible wall of energy, a kind of euphoria mixed with sheer fury.

fighting for their freedom. They poured that spirit into this incredible celebration, and I remember experiencing an overwhelming sense that they were collectively saying: 'You will *not* fucking take this away from us.'

A Part of Life

Activism isn't something that we all have the luxury of slipping in and out of. If you belong to any kind of marginalised community, it's part of your everyday life whether you say it is or not.

You might feel this burden too – if so, know it's okay to step away from conversations or move away from situations if they're exhausting you. If you don't feel up to detailing how shitty life can be for you as a misfit, you can redirect even the most well-intentioned questions to some of the handy explainers that now exist. This is also where allies are crucial: listen to marginalised people when they say they don't want to speak, and don't make them feel guilty for not doing so. We're all misfits in our own ways, so none of us are authorities on the lived experiences of *every member* of our communities. Bear this in mind, especially if you're an ally, and seek out stories and resources that can help. If you see a misfit being harassed, step in if you feel comfortable and safe to do so. Have difficult conversations with loved ones, and keep pushing to broaden their minds so that life might start to feel less challenging for future misfits to come.

Donating money is another option if you can afford to help but don't quite know how. There are amazing charities and grassroots organisations that fight tirelessly to end racism, ableism, homophobia, transphobia and misogyny, as well as human rights violations and cruel, inhumane laws. These warriors spend countless hours pouring their energy into petitions, demonstrations, advocacy and the long, decidedly unglamorous struggle for greater freedoms. These organisers are endlessly valuable, and their work is often unsung, hidden behind the scenes.

Politicised by Default

Visibility and representation are both important when it comes to broadening our horizons and humanising people who don't share our experiences, but not everyone wants to be an activist all of the time, and there is a wide-spread tendency to conflate artists from marginalised backgrounds with activists. Sometimes, this is welcomed – especially when political messages are part of the DNA of the work. But often, it's just straight-up tiresome to be politicised without ever asking or aiming to be. When your existence is politicised by default, you become an accidental activist.

A wildly talented musician who knows this feeling well is Mx Blouse, a South African artist who makes the kind of funky, infectious songs that get lodged in your head for days. Blouse is inspired by the hip-hop and kwaito (a slowed-down, chilled-out variation of house music pioneered in South Africa) they grew up with, and their lyrics – rapped in a mixture of English and Zulu, their native language – range from character-driven stories to calls to action. In 'Is'phukphuku' (which loosely translates to 'fool' in English), Blouse lays down their revolutionary potential: 'Times, they are changing / It's a revolution when someone like me has your ears when I speak.'

Don't be fooled, though – Blouse is multi-dimensional, resistant to being pigeonholed and firmly in control of their own narrative. Here, in their own words, is their story of becoming a cult superstar.

POLITICAL BODIES WITH MX BLOUSE

In 2016, when I was living in Cape Town, I went to get drunk at a friend's house. I ended up working on some music with this guy I met there, who threw parties. He started beatboxing and I started rapping along, drunk out of my mind. We made a few tracks, I put one on Soundcloud and it got picked up by a party promoter who asked me to come perform. I was like, 'Oh, shit, this is a real thing now!' Then I got booked for three shows in Germany, which was a mind-fuck – there are people listening to my music in the northern hemisphere? Are you kidding me?! I never thought of going international.

I use a lot of my indigenous language, Zulu, in my music, so people approached me after shows to ask about the lyrics. They wanted to put their meanings, their feelings into context. There were a lot of generic questions about where I come from, why I dress the way I do. Maybe people expected me to turn up in African prints? That's not a real thing – I wear black most of the time. I think it was a shock to people that there are Africans who look like me.

We are all political bodies, but I am not an activist. I think a lot of queer people get pigeonholed into that label. Activists do important work, and me being who I am in the spaces I am might be a form of activism, but I will never label myself that way. I remember, my sister brought a friend to one of my shows, and the friend's boyfriend was like, 'Wow, I didn't think queer people could rap.' What do you mean? We've got voices, we've got mouths, we can put words together!

I get a lot of interview requests, and a lot of them are just about queer identity. Lately, I've just been like, 'I won't do this.' You wouldn't call

'WE ARE ALL POLITICAL BODIES, BUT I AM NOT AN ACTIVIST.'

a male rapper and ask him to speak about being a man, so why do it to me? It's also about resisting the people who try to make me a voice or a representative for my community. I can only speak for myself, and oftentimes those attempts are all about fake inclusion anyway. Truly opening up spaces for me includes covering me the way you would any other artist, or not just booking me during Pride month. It doesn't mean just asking me for a comment whenever something horrific happens. There are actual activists to speak on that, go ask them!

I think that doing things that aren't expected of me is political enough, right? There are people who are good at the work of activism, and I support them wherever I can. I never claim that title, though. I'm an artist.

AₙGER IS ENƎRGY

Anger is unhealthy? Keep it inside? Dial it down? Bottle it up? Absolutely not. Anger is productive.

Look at the world – it's a shit-show! Wealth and privilege can cushion the blow, but everyone has their own issues to deal with – and, let's be real, the world can be fucking awful enough to tear down even the most committed optimist. Sure, it's important not to dwell on that and learn to work through those emotions so we don't get consumed by our anger, overwhelmed and pushed down into the depths of total mental misery. But don't discount your anger either; it's an important emotion.

Don't let anybody say you have no right to be angry – and more importantly, question who is *allowed* to be angry. Too often, marginalised people – people of colour, disabled people, queer and trans people – are described as 'angry' since it's a word that implies their arguments aren't logical because they're coming from a place of fury. Those who have nothing to lose in debates about human rights, and are therefore seen to be truly objective about discrimination, get to use adjectives like 'passionate' instead, while whole swathes of us worldwide feel like we need to police our reactions in order to be taken seriously.

We're quick to condemn anger, but much more reluctant to examine its roots. People around the world are fucking furious, and they've got every right to be. There is inequality, oppression and so much more. Anger tells us something needs to change. Can you imagine a history of activism without anger? From the Combahee River Collective, the Black feminists who rallied together to fight for Black women when mainstream white feminism wouldn't, to ACT UP, the queer trailblazers whose 'die-ins' and unapologetically queer slogans challenged governments' homophobic mishandling of the AIDS crisis, the history of protest simply wouldn't exist without fury.

'THE MISFIT REVOLUTION IS HERE'

The real problems develop when we don't have a healthy outlet for our feelings or can't express them. We have to communicate when we've had enough. And to push to resolve the reasons we're livid in the first place, we need to fight for a better, fairer world that welcomes and nurtures everyone. The misfit revolution is here.

WEIRDOS WIN IN THE END

It's been a wild, wacky and occasionally emotional ride, but hopefully this book has shown you once and for all that it's absolutely possible to win at life as a weirdo. You'll have shit thrown in your way because of parts of yourself that you can't change, but why would you want to change? Being a misfit brimming with brilliance in a world full of ordinary is arguably one of the greatest qualities you could ever ask for – sure I might be biased, but it worked for me and my gang of gloriously eccentric outcasts.

More than anything, I hope the lessons we've all learned and shared along the way have lit a fire in you and encouraged you to question and challenge *everything* I know that stepping off the conformist freeway and onto a slightly bumpy, haphazard lane is far from easy – speaking from experience I can say that it's fucking terrifying! But when you start following your own path on your own terms, it's better than any orgasm you'll ever experience. Lean into the chaos and smash through the fear, even it takes a little time and a carefully curated support network.

Remember your worth too, and don't settle for less. Stop trying to live in someone else's world – you *are* the mother-fucking world!

Life Lessons

Throughout the book, I've outlined again and again that the rigid constructs of society encourage us to shrink ourselves and give up on our goals. We're told that dreams – the fantasy lands, the unconventional life goals that go against the grain of what society expects – are pointless because they're not productive, but without tapping into that child-like ability to dream of a limitless world, none of us in this book would be where we are today. Frankly, the idea that we should 'get real' and 'grow up' is, in most cases, absolute bollocks. Sure, we need to learn survival skills and figure out how to navigate the world independently as adults, but the notion that we should abandon joy in favour of the shit, monotonous routines deemed the only way to go, which we often have no say in creating, is totally outrageous. Fuck That!

Throughout this journey, the ultimate goal has been to encourage you to unlock a new awareness of yourself, and to dispel any toxic myths that we misfits are unworthy of representation and ultimately destined to shrink ourselves or be stamped out by a world that hates to see us thriving. What kept me anchored – and what will hopefully do the same for you – is that what brings each of us joy is completely unique, and you're the only one who can determine and pursue what that looks and feels like for *you*.

Comparing yourself to other people might be tempting, but it's the world's most pointless exercise. It's an endless cycle of self-sabotage that ends up clouding your judgement and tricking you into chasing arbitrary ideals you probably didn't give a fuck about in the first place. Now you've begun to question things more deeply and figure out what the misfit experience looks like for you, it's time to latch onto everything you've discovered about yourself and keep checking in on those goals. Ask yourself genuinely: how are you doing? What do you want to change in the world? What are the qualities you've learned to love about yourself, and how can you keep bringing them to the fore to keep being the most brilliant misfit version of yourself possible?

This can all feel self-indulgent and even a little self-centred at times, especially in a world that's constantly, literally burning. Yet your mental health and self-esteem directly determine how much capacity you have to keep fighting, no matter what that fight looks like. Taking a break, putting yourself first and saying no to opportunities doesn't mean you've given up, it means that you've learned to preserve yourself in order to keep that glorious fire burning for longer.

If you are wondering whether you can take all of this and put it into your daily life, you absolutely can. I don't believe anyone reads a book and then transforms into a

SMASH THROUGH THE FEAR

completely different person; I might be a drag queen darling, but I'm not a bloody magician!

Yet I *do* believe that when doors to new world views open up, you can walk through them and leap right into fresh, exciting challenges. Life will continue to sling shit your way, and people will keep asking you to play by totally arbitrary, pointless rules. It's up to you to stand firm in your findings, and to hold on to your determination to reject societal norms. See the checklist below for some ways to focus on keeping to your path and moving forward.

CHECKLIST

✓ Have you got some kind of distant goal – no matter how ridiculous or tiny it might seem – in mind that *you* have determined will bring joy when you reach it?

✓ Are you making sure to check in with other magical misfits, whether online or IRL, to soak up their energy?

✓ If something scares you but you *know* the fear will be worth it, are you figuring out ways to run into it?

✓ Have you done something gloriously silly – dancing around your room, jumping into a puddle, cackling out loud at a friend's shit joke – today?

✓ Are you checking in with yourself daily and truly asking yourself if you're okay?

✓ If you aren't, are you figuring out ways to reach out for the help you need?

These are all questions that I've found nudge me gently towards that sweet, sweet serotonin on days that feel impossibly shit. Those days will still be there – life is totally unpredictable, and much as some self-help gurus may imply, there is no easy, linear path towards self-enlightenment. Fear will never leave you, no matter how fulfilled you feel; it will still linger, whether it's your colleagues saying you're 'too much' in the canteen or your mum calling you out on your outlandish dungarees! The challenge is to learn to run headfirst into it!

Beautiful Misfit Army

No matter what we see – or in too many cases, don't see – on-screen, remember you're not alone in feeling like a misfit. There will be beautiful weirdos worldwide who can relate to your experiences, whatever they may be. I've been lucky enough to drag my merry band of freaks with me throughout my chaotic journey, and there's nothing to stop you doing the same, whatever that looks like for you. There's value in seeking out other misfits and surrounding yourself with an army of like-minded outcasts, no matter how hard it might seem to track them down.

When we do find them and stand together combining all of our lessons, wobbles and kooks, we are resplendent. We lift each other up, celebrate and commiserate together. We are all interwoven and enriched by our differences, and together we fight – in our own small ways – against the banal and mundane.

My biggest goal in life – and the sole driving force behind this book – is to shine a light and connect the dots on that weirdly universal feeling of being the odd one out. Because we hold the power when we come together. If we unite, whether in real life or online, through literature, art, science or music, we can collectively form communities. Together as beautiful misfit armies, we can combine our voices to ensure we're all seen, heard and valued.

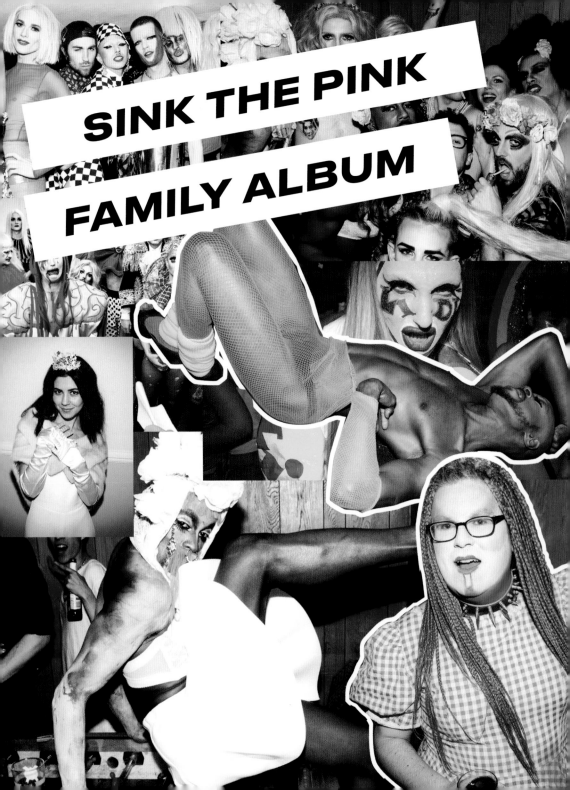

SINK THE PINK

FAMILY ALBUM

ENDNOTES

You've Got the Power

1. static1.squarespace.com/static/58c1d7399f7456c9116ad8c8/
t/5cd352044785d3e44d72abef/1557352966574/
WAD+Hair+Equality+Report+2019.pdf
2. www.independent.co.uk/news/uk/home-news/schools-ban-
hijabs-fasting-lord-agnew-government-backing-backlash-
minister-a8204876.html
3. www.reuters.com/article/us-latam-lgbt-schools-trans-
idUSKBN26S02F
4. bowenstreetpress.com/blog/2017/9/21/the-queer-queer-y-violent-
slur-or-the-language-of-liberation
5. www.qrd.org/qrd/misc/text/queers.read.this
6. www.researchgate.net/publication/304035431_Role_Models

Dream Big

1 Dabiri, Emma. *What White People Can Do Next*, Penguin Books,
UK, 2021.
2 www.pinknews.co.uk/2020/02/04/gaming-industry-census-report-
lgbt-raise-the-game-uk-games-industry-diversity/
3 www.wired.com/story/how-afrofuturism-can-help-the-world-mend/

Sticks and Stones

1 www.vox.com/2015/2/16/8031073/what-are-microaggressions
2 acamh.onlinelibrary.wiley.com/doi/10.1111/jcpp.12841
3. cyberbullying.org/2019-cyberbullying-data
4. raceequalityfoundation.org.uk/wp-content/uploads/2020/03/
mental-health-report-v5-2.pdf
5. www.stonewall.org.uk/system/files/lgbt_in_britain_health.pdf
6. theconversation.com/blackout-tuesday-the-black-square-is-a-
symbol-of-online-activism-for-non-activists-139982

Chase Your Joy

1. Ben-Shahar, Dr Tal. *Happier: Can You Learn to Be Happy*? McGraw-Hill Education, UK, 2008.
2. wearesocial.com/uk/blog/2021/01/digital-2021-the-latest-insights-into-the-state-of-digital/

Find Your Tribe

1. www.nytimes.com/2016/04/21/nyregion/before-the-stonewall-riots-there-was-the-sip-in.html
2. indie-mag.com/2018/10/casa-susanna-book/
3. www.gov.uk/government/statistics/hate-crime-england-and-wales-2019-to-2020/hate-crime-england-and-wales-2019-to-2020
4. www.theguardian.com/world/2021/jun/14/us-trans-transgender-deaths-2021
5. sciencedirect.com/science/article/pii/S0028390821000721
6. socialsciences.ucla.edu/wp-content/uploads/2021/04/UCLA-Hollywood-Diversity-Report-2021-Film-4-22-2021.pdf
7. www.insider.com/lashana-lynch-coping-backlash-first-black-female-007-james-bond-2020-11
8. socialsciences.ucla.edu/hollywood-diversity-report-2020/
9. metro.co.uk/2020/07/27/david-harewood-says-black-actors-leave-uk-there-isnt-industry-support-us-13044579/
10. www.theguardian.com/stage/2021/jul/12/gina-yashere-on-riches-racism-and-us-success-i-dont-like-to-boast-but-im-doing-very-well
11. combaheerivercollective.weebly.com/the-combahee-river-collective-statement.html

Start a Revolution

1. Graeber, David. *The Utopia of Rules: On Technology, Stupidity and the Secret Joys of Bureaucracy*, Melville House Publishing, New York and London, 2015.
2. www.theguardian.com/world/ng-interactive/2021/jan/25/how-the-arab-spring-unfolded-a-visualisation
3. www.newyorker.com/culture/cultural-comment/the-second-act-of-social-media-activism

RESOURCES AND RECOMMENDATIONS

Support Hotlines

UK
Mind
www.mind.org.uk // 0300 123 3393
A mental health charity dedicated to improving services, raising awareness and supporting those in need of mental health support.

National Bullying Helpline
www.nationalbullyinghelpline.co.uk // 0300 323 0169
The UK's only charity to directly address bullying, whether online or in person.

Samaritans
www.samaritans.org // 116 123
A UK-based charity offering support on everything from mental illness to workplace support.

Shout
www.giveusashout.org // 85285
A mental health text messaging support line – text 85285 in the UK to access support.

Switchboard LGBT
www.switchboard.lgbt // 020 7837 6768
A confidential mental health hotline staffed by LGBTQ+ professionals.

US
National Alliance on Mental Health
www.nami.org // 1-800-950-6264
A US-wide advocacy group founded by family members of people living with mental illness.

National Suicide Prevention Lifeline
www.suicidepreventionlifeline.org // 1-800-273-8255
A free, confidential hotline for people in distress. Also offers crisis resources and best-practice guidelines for professionals.

The Trevor Project
www.thetrevorproject.org // (866) 488-7386
The world's largest suicide prevention and crisis intervention organisation for LGBTQ+ youth.

Charities / NGOs

UK
AKT
www.akt.org.uk
An LGBTQ+ youth homelessness charity offering support and access to emergency resources.

Autism Plus
www.autismplus.co.uk
An organisation that supports adults across the UK with autism, learning disabilities, mental health conditions and complex needs.

Black Minds Matter UK
www.blackmindsmatteruk.com
A UK-based charity connecting Black individuals to mental health resources.

Not a Phase
notaphase.org
Supporting the lives of trans+ adults through awareness campaigning, developing company diversity strategies and supporting trans+ owned projects.

Stonewall
www.stonewall.org.uk
The UK's largest LGBTQ+ charity, offers resources and advice.

Stonewall Housing
stonewallhousing.org
Helping LGBTQ+ people to find safe spaces and secure homes.

US
American Association of People with Disabilities
www.aapd.com
A nationwide US organisation fighting for the rights of people with disabilities.

Black Lives Matter
blacklivesmatter.com
A global organisation working to liberate Black communities worldwide.

GLITS Inc
www.glitsinc.org
A US-based organisation offering key harm reduction services to trans communities across the country.

Books
***The Body Keeps the Score: Mind, Brain and Body in the Transformation of Trauma* by Bessel van der Kolk (Penguin Books, 2015)**
A comprehensively researched guide on understanding, managing and healing from trauma.

***Fattily Ever After* by Stephanie Yeboah (Hardie Grant Books, 2020)**
A guide to living life unapologetically, written from the perspective of a Black, plus-sized woman.

***Release the Beast* by Bimini (Viking, 2021)**
A conversational eye-opening guide to life written through the lens of a non-binary drag artist.

***The Transgender Issue* by Shon Faye (Allen Lane, 2021)**
Driven by radical politics, this polemic outlines the daily realities of life as a trans person in the UK.

***What Doesn't Kill You* by Tessa Miller (Henry Holt & Company, 2021)**
A touching memoir full of guidance for those navigating life with chronic illness.

***Reasons to Stay Alive* by Matt Haig (Canongate Books, 2015)**
A memoir written from the perspective of surviving mental illness.

Talks and Lectures

Michaela Coel's James MacTaggart
Lecture, Edinburgh TV Festival 2018
www.youtube.com/
watch?v=odusP8gmqsg
A speech on the realities of navigating
creative industries as a misfit, and
learning to own your power.

TED Talk: The Beauty of Being a Misfit
www.youtube.com/
watch?v=9AgCr2tTvng
A talk by Lidia Yuknavitch about loss,
shame and self-acceptance, all through
the lens of embracing life as a misfit.

TED Talk: The Power of Introverts
www.youtube.com/
watch?v=c0KYU2j0TM4
A vital critique of society's privileging
of extroversion, and a manifesto for
introverts worldwide.

Podcasts

I Weigh with Jameela Jamil
Stories about mental health, social
activism and challenging the norms of
the world.

The Last Bohemians
A series of audio portraits and interviews
with some of history's most fascinating,
fearless women.

Maintenance Phase
A hilarious, historical podcast which
debunks myths throughout the global
history of diet culture.

Campaigners on Instagram

@cozcon
An illustrator whose work centres
on Black, trans liberation.

@gemmacorrell
British cartoonist Gemma illustrates
her life with anxiety, social fears
and pugs.

@hellomynameiswednesday
Wednesday is a non-binary artist
whose colourful, joyous portraits
communicate messages of self-love
and self-acceptance.

@meganjaynecrabbe
A body-empowerment campaigner who
believes we are all good enough as
we are.

ABOUT THE AUTHOR

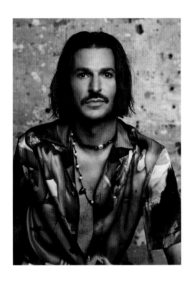

Over the last ten years, Glyn Fussell has cemented himself as the King of the UK club scene. It all started over a decade ago when he and his best friend came up with the idea of what made the perfect night out. And so the cultural phenomenon Sink The Pink was born, one of the biggest, most innovative nights out in the UK, which has sold out venues across the UK. He is also co-founder of the festival Mighty Hoopla, which continues to provide safe spaces for the LGBTQ+ community.

Based in London, Glyn is a creative force of nature and poster boy for all misfits, putting diversity, inclusion, colour and fun at the heart of everything he touches. This LGBTQ+ trailblazer works to push the community forward by giving opportunities and spaces for marginalised people to thrive and succeed. As well as this, Glyn a trustee for Not a Phase and Stonewall Housing and is a long-time fundraiser for LGBTQ+ charities.

Also a broadcaster, Glyn is the host of *Drag Queens' Den* for Radio 1 on BBC Sounds, a podcast in which he discusses his drag expertise alongside queens and celebrity fans from across the country. It is a huge step in the right direction on Glyn's mission to uplift the crossover of LGBTQ+ spaces and the mainstream.

He is loud and proud, a man with many strings to his bow and an infectious personality.

@glynfussell

ABOUT SINK THE PINK

Sink The Pink is the largest LGBTQ+ collective and club night in the UK, continually challenging the status quo around nightlife culture and celebrating freedom of self-expression. At Sink The Pink, everyone is welcome and everyone is celebrated.

Founded in 2008, Sink The Pink began as a response to 'too many bland and non-inclusive nights out'. Growing from humble beginnings in a working men's club in East London, Sink The Pink now tour the world with their legendary parties, live performances and immersive productions. Their dedication to diversity, creativity and joy has attracted communities and audiences from across the globe.

Sink The Pink is a melting pot of drag artists, club kids, performers, decorated choreographers, creatives and acclaimed set and costume designers. Inspired by theatre, dance, punk, pop culture and fashion, they are the antidote to the new wave of soulless mega-clubs. They perform on famous stages around the world, as well as collaborating with artists such as Little Mix, Pink, Melanie C and Years & Years, along with an array of international brands and charities who support equality.

sinkthepink.com / @sink_the_pink

'Sink The Pink are the gender-fucking drag collective changing London.'
Dazed

'Colourful and transgressive, the club that's saving queer nightlife.'
The Guardian

'Sink The Pink are the people putting on the best parties in London and dissolving gender stereotypes.'
Wonderland

ABOUT THE CONTRIBUTORS

LILY ALLEN

London-born Lily Allen is a singer, songwriter and actress with multiple top 10 singles and four studio albums under her belt, as well as a lead role in the West End play *2:22 A Ghost Story*. She has headlined at Mighty Hoopla and performed on stage at Sink The Pink, and her fresh and candid words have often given voice to important issues.
www.lilyallenmusic.com

JONBENET BLONDE

The self-described 'elusive chanteuse of East London drag', JonBenet moved from Northern Ireland to London more than a decade ago, and has since modelled for the likes of Agent Provocateur and YSL Beauty. A long-time member of the Sink The Pink family, JonBenet has also walked the runway for designers such as Bobby Abley and has been photographed by fashion photography royalty.
jonbersblonde.com

MELANIE C

Also known as Sporty Spice, Melanie C is a world-renowned recording artist with more than 108 million records sold worldwide. At just 22 years old, the Liverpool-born star joined chart-topping girl group the Spice Girls, releasing three albums before disbanding in 2000. Since then, Melanie has had continued solo success and has toured the world with Sink The Pink, earning her stripes as a high-profile LGBTQ+ ally.
melaniec.net

ROSIE JONES

Rosie Jones is a renowned comedian, actress and scriptwriter born in Bridlington, England. As well as touring extensively, Rosie has featured on various prime-time comedy panel shows and co-written an episode of Netflix series *Sex Education*. Rosie often applies her sharp wit to her own disability, cracking jokes about her cerebral palsy. In media interviews throughout the years, she has also advocated for disability rights and called for greater queer and disabled representation in media and pop culture more generally.
rosiejonescomedy.com

LADY PHYLL

Phyllis Akua Opoku-Gyimah, better known as Lady Phyll, is a British LGBTQ+ activist and co-founder of UK Black Pride, Europe's largest celebration for African, Asian, Middle Eastern, Latin American and Caribbean heritage LGBTQ+ people. Phyll is also a committed trade unionist and a former trustee of UK LGBTQ+ charity Stonewall – a role which she stepped down from in 2019, when Stonewall and UK Black Pride officially partnered. Phyll turned down an MBE in 2016, but has earned

countless accolades – in October 2020, she was named on a list of 100 Great Black Britons.
linktr.ee/ladyphyll

GINNY LEMON

Named after their fondness of gin and their 'zesty' performances, British-born Ginny Lemon is a drag performer best known for their stint on Season 2 of *RuPaul's Drag Race UK*, as well as their appearance on *The X Factor* in 2017. A charismatic performer with an acid-hued wardrobe, Ginny is also a musician with a reputation for singing live vocals at their drag shows.
@ginnylemon69

RAVEN MANDELLA

Born and raised in Chapeltown, Leeds, Raven Mandella is a multi-talented DJ, dancer, choreographer and drag queen known for travelling the world and working with everyone from Kelly Rowland to Nile Rodgers. As well as being part of the core Sink The Pink family, Raven is the founder of the House of Mandella and a former ambassador for Glitterbox Ibiza.
@raven_mandella

JAY BARRY MATTHEWS

Australian-born Jay Barry Matthews is a self-described 'catwalking, non-binary queer activist' and a creative powerhouse responsible for some of Sink The Pink's most fabulous looks. A bona fide drag legend in their own right, Jay created the 'Drag Energy Embodiment' workshop, which teaches how to harness the potential of drag to smash through barriers in everyday life.
@jaybarrymatthews / @jazbazmaz

MX BLOUSE

Mx Blouse is a genre-defying musician and creative polymath born in Melmoth, a small town in South Africa. After years spent working in consumer trends research and arts journalism, Blouse began to experiment with music and later released a debut EP in 2017. A handful of other releases and collaborations, most notably with Berlin-based, South-Africa-born electronic music producer Thor Rixon, have followed, earning Blouse a global fanbase and a reputation as a truly forward-thinking artist.
@sandiblouse

AMY REDMOND

Amy Redmond is a Margate-based festival director and co-founder of Sink The Pink. With a background as a BBC radio producer, Redmond has spent the last five years building queer community organisations in Margate, as well as co-founding Margate Arts Club. In 2016, she co-founded Margate Pride and has since transformed it from a small event with around 500 attendees to a bona fide phenomenon, with more than 10,000 in annual attendance. In 2019, she was appointed Artistic Director of POW! Thanet, an arts and culture festival and charity celebrating feminism, women and girls. @missamyzing

GRACE SHUSH

A former Miss Sink The Pink contest winner, Grace Shush is a charismatic drag queen and close member of the Sink The Pink family. Grace is also a skilled host, podcaster and DJ, whose past clients include ASOS, MTV, E4 and John Lewis. They describe their drag in a nutshell as a 'hyper-sexualised, bearded Adele'.
@graceshushh

SKIN

Skin is the stage name of Deborah Anne Dyer OBE, a London-born singer, songwriter and DJ best known as the lead vocalist of British rock band Skunk Anansie. Formed in 1994, the band quickly found acclaim for their hard, edgy sound and unashamedly political lyrics, before disbanding for the first time in 2001. Skin released a series of solo albums before the group reformed in 2009. Not only has Skin been vocal about the difficulties of being accepted as a young, Black woman in rock, she has also championed various charitable causes – and in 2017, the Skunk Anansie Scholarship was founded to financially support aspiring musicians.
www.skinmusic.com

DANI ST JAMES

Born in Barry, a small town in the south of Wales, Dani St James is a renowned trans model, activist and co-founder of Not a Phase, a registered charity supporting the lives of trans adults across the UK. For the last decade, Dani has worked various jobs in make-up and nightlife before building a substantial following online, which she uses to discuss the obstacles facing trans communities. Not a Phase continues to do vital work both publicly and behind the scenes, devising diversity strategies for companies and supporting trans-owned businesses across the UK.
@danistjames

JADE THIRLWALL

Born and raised in South Shields, England, Jade Thirlwall shot to fame in 2011 as a founding member of world-famous girl group Little Mix. Since ascending the ranks of UK talent show *The X Factor*, Little Mix has gone on to become one of the best-selling girl groups worldwide, having sold more than 60 million records over the last decade. Jade is also a vocal LGBTQ+ ally, using her social media platforms to champion causes close to her heart.
@jadethirlwall

YUNGBLUD

Ever since the release of his debut, self-titled EP in 2018, Yungblud – the stage name of Doncaster-born recording artist Dominic Harrison – has earned acclaim for his unique brand of twenty-first-century pop punk, which also takes inspiration from emo rock and rap. Known for his androgynous look and high-octane performance style, Yungblud's albums have topped charts worldwide and featured lyrics about issues such as sexual assault, individualism and mental health awareness.
www.yungbludofficial.com

ACKNOWLEDGEMENTS

Wow I can't believe that I am finally giving birth to this book! It's taken a TEAM to get here so here goes…

Charlotte, you made my dreams come true. No amount of avocados could ever repay you. THANKS from the bottom of my heart.

Zoe Ross – you absolute queen, thanks for not giving up on this idea and guiding it to the perfect place. LOVE.

Jake Hall – raise a glass and whack on some Marina, We did it!!! Thanks for your love, patience and cuddles, I adore you and you pushed this further than I ever dreamt it could go.

Zara, Laura, Lewis, Jess and the entire White Lion team, thanks for pushing me, challenging me and supporting all my ideas, you have been a dream and I hope this is just the beginning of a magical future.

All my East Creative family, Craig in particular – superstar.

My family and my chosen family – I am so grateful for you all, apologies if I have been a nightmare whilst creating this.

To the STP family – wow we have achieved so many insane things together, thanks for constantly inspiring me, corrupting me and making me live in full technicolour.

To all my contributors – you have no idea how much it means that you shared your stories and I love you so much for that.

Amy and Jamie – THANKS for lifting me up and always sticking with me.

And finally My Jim….I LOVE YOU.